A SHORT HISTORY OF THE 1916 RISING

A SHORT HISTORY OF THE 1916 RISING

RICHARD KILLEEN

Gill & Macmillan

Gill & Macmillan Ltd
Hume Avenue, Park West, Dublin 12
with associated companies throughout the world
www.gillmacmillan.ie

Index compiled by Cover To Cover
Typography design by Make Communication
Print origination by Síofra Murphy
Map supplied by Arcadia Editions Limited
Printed by GraphyCems Ltd, Spain

This book is typeset in Minion 11pt on 14pt.

The paper used in this book comes from the wood pulp of
managed forests. For every tree felled, at least one tree is
planted, thereby renewing natural resources.

A CIP catalogue record is available for this book
from the British Library.

5 4 3 2

CONTENTS

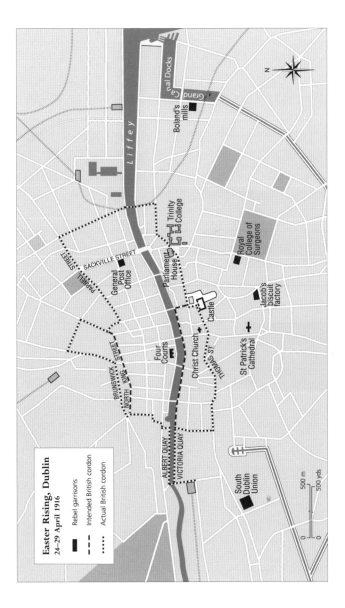

Easter Rising, Dublin
24–29 April 1916

■ Rebel garrisons
- - - Intended British cordon
····· Actual British cordon

Grand Canal Docks

Liffey

Boland's mills

Trinity College

PARNELL STREET

SACKVILLE STREET

General Post Office

Parliament House

Castle

Royal College of Surgeons

Jacob's biscuit factory

BRUNSWICK STREET

NORTH KING STREET

Four Courts

Christ Church

THOMAS ST.

St Patrick's Cathedral

ALBERT QUAY

VICTORIA QUAY

South Dublin Union

N

0   500 m
0   500 yds

INTRODUCTION

Rising or rebellion? What's in a name? The events of Easter Week 1916 have been denominated under both headings. 'Rising' is generally preferred by those who see 1916 as the heroic foundation moment of Irish independence. 'Rebellion' is more ambiguous, for the word 'rebel' is no pejorative in the Irish revolutionary tradition. That most republican of counties, Cork, proudly assumes the epithet for itself. Yet rebellion can also mean an illegal challenge to lawful authority. When a properly constituted state, whose integrity is acknowledged in international law, harbours minority or regional groups which seek to secede from or otherwise subvert its integrity, such groups are usually referred to as rebels. Think of the Tamil Tigers in Sri Lanka or of ETA in the Basque Country. But then, if treason prosper none dare call it treason: the quondam rebels, if successful, become founding fathers. Rebellion can then be worn as a badge of honour, its actions sanctified as a rising. Mind you, further manifestations of the rebel spirit—if directed at the new order—tend to get snuffed out without much sentiment. Think Cuba, or the Irish civil war.

I have chosen the word 'rising' in the title of this book, not because I think Easter Week was a foundation moment in the long-established cause of Irish independence but because it decisively—and for the most part successfully—changed the course of that struggle. It gave Irish nationalism a new grammar and a new vision of practical possibility. The state that emerged in nationalist Ireland in 1922 was of a nature that could hardly be imagined before the rising, when autonomy within the United Kingdom represented the settled consensual demand of most Irish nationalists. The various minorities of Fenians, Sinn Féiners, Irish-Irelanders and cultural separatists who dreamed of surging beyond the home rule consensus were marginal to the overall national project. In 1912, they were merely an important part of the nationalist coalition, a kind of internal radical opposition. Ten years later, they were the new elite. In 1912, John Redmond was the undisputed leader of Irish nationalism. Ten years later, he was dead, forgotten and discounted.

The events of Easter Week 1916 were central to this sea change. The rising did not create the independent Irish state, but it created the conditions that allowed it to assume the form that it took six years later. Those who argue that there was really little to choose between the 1914 Home Rule Act and the Anglo-Irish Treaty of 1921 are wrong. Under home rule the flag would have been the Union Jack and the anthem 'God Save the King'. The degree of financial autonomy would have been less and the capacity to build the full institutional apparatus of an independent state would have been withheld.

Ireland would have been a different place without 1916. I don't just mean nationalist Ireland. The rising did not lead directly to partition, a subject that had been on

the British political radar at least as early as May 1912
when the Liberal backbench MP, T.C. Agar-Robertes,
moved an unsuccessful amendment to Asquith's Home
Rule Bill to exclude the four counties of Derry, Down,
Antrim and Armagh from its provisions. But by
ratcheting up the nationalist demand, it made partition
ever more likely. If unionist Ulster strained at the gnat of
home rule, it was never going to swallow the camel of a
republic.

And a republic was what eventually issued from the
process set in motion by the events of Easter Week. It
was a constitutionally ambiguous beast at first, not
formally calling itself a republic until 1949. It subsisted
from 1922 merely as a Free State as declared in the Treaty
and then, in de Valera's 1937 constitution, as 'a sovereign,
independent, democratic' state from which all reference
to the British crown was finally removed. The eventual
declaration of the republic in 1949 was a kind of relief all
round, for de Valera had effectively legitimised
republican institutions during his sixteen-year rule
following 1932. In the context of that overwhelming
legitimacy, the nationalist population inevitably looked
back to the republican rising as the foundation of the
new reality.

To contemporaries of the event, more alert to its
ambiguities than their children were to be, it was nearly
always the rebellion. The glorious late spring weather
that marked the week was referred to years later by old
timers as 'rebellion weather'. One of the most valuable
contemporary sources for our knowledge of the rising

was the *Sinn Fein Rebellion Handbook* published by the *Irish Times* in 1917. The use of the word 'rebellion' reflected ordinary contemporary usage (as did the erroneous and unaccented reference to Sinn Féin) rather than the *Irish Times*' political bias, although there could be little doubt on that latter score. It was also the reason advanced by the late Max Caulfield for using the word in the title of his history, *The Easter Rebellion*, first published in the 1960s and based substantially on interviews with surviving witnesses and participants. Even the best modern survey, Charles Townshend's *Easter 1916*, employs the term 'rebellion' because 'it contains the term for its makers, and that term—"rebels"—carries a charge of romantic glamour which was wholly appropriate to their minds'.

The word 'rising' was never completely absent: James Stephens' indispensable eye-witness account, *The Insurrection in Dublin*, written contemporaneously and published only months after the event, provides the earliest non-partisan use of the term that I can find. In the foreword, he declares that 'the few chapters that make up this book are not a history of the rising'. But throughout the short book, Stephens prefers the term 'insurrection', as in his title. The popularisation of the term 'rising' came later, with the triumphal assertion of Easter Week as the foundation moment of the new, republican Ireland. It is because of the validity of that observation, rather than because of its triumphal quality, that I choose 'rising'—carefully and appropriately lower case—for this short book.

All this verbal shilly-shallying hints at the contested nature of Easter Week as an historical event. It was indeed a foundation moment, but the building is—in the eyes of many—unfinished. Whether it is actually unfinished, or alternatively whether it can ever be finished, or again whether it would be desirable to do so, is another day's work. But Easter 1916 did leave unfinished business in the eyes of many, and Northern Ireland suffered over thirty years of misery in an attempt to finish it. On the other hand, the Republic of Ireland, the institutional child of the rising, has demonstrated no urgent desire to extend its house and seems to regard the present building as a neat, snug edifice altogether. The alacrity with which its citizens voted away the state's constitutional claim to the territory of Northern Ireland in 1998 was instructive.

In the end, there is the event itself. All else is remembering and interpretation. What follows is a narrative of the event, with as much and as little explanatory context as is required to give meaning to that narrative.

RK
Dublin, February 2009

01 | FENIANS

In September 1898, the last prisoner was released. Tom Clarke had spent fifteen years in Millbank, Chatham and Portland prisons for his part in the dynamite campaign of the 1880s. The charge had been treason-felony and Clarke had endured the savage prison regime reserved for those convicted of it. Two of the other three convicted with him on 14 June 1883, Dr Thomas Gallagher and John J. Murphy, went insane.

The dynamite campaign is one of the less remembered episodes in the story of militant Irish nationalism. In the wake of the abortive rising of 1867, a new secret society was formed in New York. Called Clan na Gael (the Family of the Gaels), its purpose was to revive the damaged fortunes of the organisation in whose name the rising had been launched. The Irish Republican

Brotherhood (IRB) had been founded in 1858 simultaneously with a sister organisation in the United States, the Fenian Brotherhood. In effect, the two bodies were one. The word 'Fenian' was derived from a heroic warrior band celebrated in Irish mythology.

The fiasco of 1867 left the IRB/Fenians low in the water. The situation in Ireland was hopeless for the moment, so the best and only opportunity to revive militant fortunes lay across the Atlantic. This was the role assumed by Clan na Gael.

The Clan quickly established itself as the most vigorous and successful of Irish-American political bodies. Its influence was to be felt back in Ireland continuously from its foundation right up to the beginning of World War II. It was the product of the huge post-Famine emigration from Ireland, which saw the island's population drop from 8.2 million in 1841 to 4.4 million in 1911. The emigrants who landed in the United States brought with them a profound bitterness and hatred towards Britain, which they blamed for the horrors of the Famine. It was from this population that the Clan drew its strength, attracting energetic and driven men.

By the 1880s, the Clan had come under the influence of a trio known simply as the Triangle. Although opposed by the formal leadership, the Triangle had sufficient influence to mount a campaign which would take the fight for Irish freedom back across the ocean, not to Ireland but to the very heart of the imperial British state. Their weapon of choice was dynamite.

Dynamite had been invented by the Swedish chemist Alfred Nobel in 1866, so it was a fairly novel tool of war by the time the Triangle had the idea of putting it to use in Britain. They were not alone in the world in appreciating its potential. Revolutionaries in late-Tsarist Russia also resorted to dynamite from the 1880s onward. But for Britain at the height of its imperial afternoon, it was a rude shock. Bombs destroyed a gasholder in Glasgow; there were attacks on the London Underground system and in railway stations; a bomb damaged Scotland Yard itself; the Tower of London was attacked. Most dramatically, the dynamiters threw a bomb into the chamber of the House of Commons itself, causing a lot of damage. Through a mixture of incompetence and good luck, relatively few people died in the dynamite war. The Irish-American groups were traced by the police and by 1885 the four-year campaign was at an end.

It was for his part in all this that Tom Clarke was imprisoned. Clarke had been born on the Isle of Wight, the son of an Irishman serving in the British army, in 1858. He was coeval with the Fenians themselves. After a childhood spent partly in South Africa and partly in Ireland, he emigrated to the United States at twenty-one years of age and promptly joined Clan na Gael. Assuming the alias of Henry Hammond Wilson, he was part of a dynamite team led by Dr Thomas Gallagher. His alias remained secure until after his conviction, although he had the private pleasure of giving the police his occupation as 'clerk'.

Patrick Pearse addressing a meeting in the Dublin suburb of Dolphin's Barn, 1915. (*Courtesy of the National Library of Ireland*)

Eventually released after fifteen years, Clarke was promptly rewarded with the Freedom of the City of Limerick but not with employment. He returned to the United States for eight years before coming back to Ireland in 1907 to open a newsagents and tobacconists shop, financed from his American savings, at 75A Great Britain Street (now Parnell Street) in the centre of Dublin and another in nearby Amiens Street. He was now almost fifty years old, married into the Dalys, an influential Fenian family from Limerick, and himself an unrepentant Fenian.

But what did it mean to be a Fenian, unrepentant or otherwise? Who were the Fenians?

———

The traditional view of Irish nationalism is that it comprised a majority constitutional wing, focused on a reform programme at Westminster which would ultimately deliver home rule, and a militant, republican minority uninterested in parliamentary politics and dedicated only to the overthrow of British rule in Ireland by force of arms. In this binary division, the militants were the Fenians—more or less. This is a caricature, although like all caricatures it contains a likeness.

By the last quarter of the nineteenth century, nationalism had effectively developed into the organised political project of the Irish Catholic community. Notwithstanding the fact that its most dramatic and successful leader, Charles Stewart Parnell, was a Protestant, the vast majority of Irish Nationalist MPs at Westminster were Catholics; the ever widening electorate that sent them there was overwhelmingly Catholic; and in Ulster, where sectarian divisions were blatant, every parliamentary constituency with a Catholic majority returned a Nationalist candidate and every one with a Protestant majority a Unionist. This was consistently the case in each general election from 1885 until partition in 1920.

Within the big nationalist tent, however, there were class tensions. The parliamentarians were the products of the Catholic mercantile and professional classes, sustained by support from the hierarchy, itself drawn from the same strata of the community. None of this is surprising: it was an age when wealth and land were pre-requisites for political participation. Likewise, only the educated minority could enter the professions or the higher reaches of the Church.

The Fenians were drawn from the ranks of the excluded. They were urban, lower middle class, literate and resentful. Their project was implicitly republican and populist. It reposed no confidence in the hierarchs of the parliamentary tradition or in their cousins, the bishops, who returned their hostility with interest. Between the rising of 1867 and the ascent of Parnell in the late 1870s, the Fenians were simply the largest political force in nationalist Ireland.

Parnell's genius transformed that world. The so-called New Departure of 1879 meant a functional union of the

Thomas J. Clarke. (*Courtesy of the National Library of Ireland*)

Irish Parliamentary Party, the Fenians and the recently formed Land League in a joint campaign for agrarian reform. It was a campaign that proved spectacularly successful in less than a generation. It might also be regarded as the neutering of Fenianism itself, which is correct up to a point. Equally, it injected Fenian sensibility into the party: a significant number of Parnell's MPs were or had been of the movement. The progressive widening of the franchise helped this process, enabling the lower reaches of the middle class to enter parliament.

The IRB, whose primary purpose was political, merely loaned itself to the agrarian campaign. It then had to watch Parnell drive nationalist political fortunes in parliament to a new height in 1886, when he converted Gladstone to home rule. All this, plus the manifest failure of the dynamite war, pushed Fenianism towards the margins. It still found a toehold in populist, voluntary associations, most importantly in the newly-formed Gaelic Athletic Association (1884) and in the emerging trade union movement.

The fall of Parnell brought no immediate dividend to the Fenians, as one might have expected it to do. But the populist, republican sensibility was still there, together with a belief that force of arms was more likely to deliver real results than parliamentary temporising. The IRB played a leading part in celebrating the centenary of the 1798 rising—to all republicans, the fountainhead of their tradition—but its numbers were weakened by internal dissentions and the gradual revival of the Irish Party under John Redmond from 1900 on.

By the time Tom Clarke returned from America in 1907, things looked grim for the Fenians. Redmond was regarded as the uncontested leader of Irish nationalism. Other, younger groups such as the early Sinn Féin and the Gaelic League had been born and offered a fresher alternative for those weary or suspicious of the parliamentarians. The Fenians seemed passé. When Clarke came back, the IRB had been reduced to a rump of barely a thousand members.

What followed was a partial restoration of the IRB's fortunes, driven by Clarke and younger members such as Bulmer Hobson and Sean Mac Diarmada. The latter was a classic Fenian: formal education only to primary level and thereafter largely self-educated through night classes. He became a full-time organiser for the IRB in 1908 and proved his worth at it. His preferred use of the Irish-language form of his name betrayed a generational change in Irish nationalism generally. The Gaelic League (1893) had proved a major influence for cultural change. The older generation of Fenians like Clarke were largely indifferent to language and culture, focusing exclusively on politics. Younger men like Mac Diarmada were not.

In the years up to the outbreak of World War I, the various strands of nationalist opinion outside the broad church of the Irish Party gradually converged. Gaelic Leaguers, Sinn Féin, the IRB, the GAA and other groups came to share a sense of greater urgency and possibility about the nationalist demand. The IRB's militant republicanism was only one element in this coalition of the excluded, but it was to prove critical in Easter Week.

By 1910, Redmond was at the height of his influence. The Irish Party held the balance of power at Westminster. The result was the Third Home Rule Bill of 1912. It caused uproar in Ulster, where the local Protestant majority grew hysterical at the thought of domestic domination by southern Catholics. The authorities turned a blind eye to the formation of an illegal militia, the Ulster Volunteer Force, and their importation of arms from Germany. The opposition Conservative Party, in a spectacular act of treason, supported their threatened defiance of the coming home rule legislation. There was talk of partition but for the moment it came to nothing. A threat to use the British army at the Curragh, Co. Kildare, to coerce Ulster faltered when some of the officers effectively mutinied and refused to execute the order. It was the most serious such breach of discipline in the forces of the crown since 1688.

In response to the formation of the UVF in Belfast, the Irish Volunteers were founded in Dublin in November 1913. The IRB was an element, but only an element, in the new force. Clan na Gael in America supplied the necessary funds and, just like the UVF, they imported arms from Germany. Unlike the northern authorities' complaisance, there was no blind eye turned in Dublin. An attempt was made to disarm the Volunteers. It failed,

The O'Donovan Rossa funeral committee. De Valera is third left, back row; Arthur Griffith seventh left, centre row; John MacBride is second right, centre row; Tom Clarke is eighth left, second row. (*Kilmainham Gaol Collection*)

leading to British troops being derided on the streets of Dublin. Their response left four civilians dead.

The legitimacy of British rule in Ireland was loosening. Inevitably, this had consequences for Redmond and the Irish Party, whose every hope was focused on Westminster. Nothing, it seemed, could cut the Gordian Knot of Ulster resistance which had such influential support at the very heart of the British Establishment. There were endless meetings, discussions, proposals, conferences, all to no avail. The irresistible force of home rule had met the immoveable object of Ulster. Redmond had taken Irish nationalism to what was supposed to be the mountaintop, but the way to the Promised Land was barred.

For the Fenians and the rest of the nationalist radicals in the Irish Volunteers, the frustrated home rule settlement seemed less a Promised Land than a half-way house. But for the moment, Redmond's hold on the nationalist population seemed secure, if less secure than hitherto.

Then World War I broke out.

02 | PREPARATIONS

When the war broke out, the Home Rule Act of 1914 was passed only to be suspended for the duration of the conflict. It would never see the light of day, for by the end of the war the whole world would be transformed and Ireland with it.

There was an inconsistency at the heart of the home rule project. It wished to withdraw Ireland from the British metropolitan state in national and local matters while retaining the island's presence in imperial matters. In effect, it looked two ways at once. If the greater emphasis was on domestic autonomy, the imperial minor key should not be forgotten either. The home rule elite foresaw themselves as full shareholders in the future of the British Empire, rather in the manner of the Scots elite. Indeed, given Scotland's very substantial difference to England—in the Church settlement, in law and education—the home rule imperial dream was perhaps not as fanciful as it now seems.

At all events, Redmond felt a sense of obligation to the Empire and to what was now the British war effort. In a world in which the destruction of the British Empire seemed unimaginable, this made a certain sense. After all, if home rule were achieved it would represent an internal settlement of the Irish question within the United Kingdom. One way or the other, the union flag would fly in Ireland. And now, in the autumn of 1914, that flag was a war standard. How could Redmond not support the war without exposing himself to the charge levelled at home rulers by their opponents for years: that home rule was just camouflage for outright separation?

It was a tricky position to be in and it would have required a more adroit politician than Redmond to handle it. He was shrewd enough to refuse a place in the war cabinet but he then overplayed his hand badly by calling on Irishmen to volunteer for the British army 'wherever the firing line extends'. Like many, perhaps he thought the whole thing would be over by Christmas. The effect of his call was to split the Irish Volunteers, over which he had secured nominal control. The great majority, up to 150,000 men, took Redmond's side and now styled themselves the National Volunteers. They went on to form the backbone of the two Irish regiments raised especially for war and of the 35,000 who never came back.

The dissident minority under Eoin MacNéill, a history professor and the catalyst for the foundation of the

Patrick Pearse delivering his famous oration at the grave of O'Donovan Rossa, 1915. (*Courtesy of the National Library of Ireland*)

original Volunteers the previous November, retained the iconic name of Irish Volunteers. Their number was no more than 12,000, less than 8 per cent of the original force. But it was they, or rather a further minority among them, who precipitated the Easter Rising. The Irish Volunteers later mutated into the Irish Republican Army (IRA), which in 1922 further split along the lines of the Anglo-Irish Treaty with the majority becoming the national army of the new Free State and the minority of enragés continuing a vestigial existence as the IRA. They would, of course, be heard from again in more recent times.

In September 1914, when the Volunteers split, MacNéill's dissenting minority declared that 'Ireland cannot, with honour or safety, take part in foreign quarrels other than through the free action of a national government of her own.' The signatories of this document included names that would be prominent in Easter Week: Patrick Pearse, Thomas MacDonagh, Joseph Plunkett, Eamonn Ceannt, Sean Mac Diarmada and The O'Rahilly. None of them survived the rising. The first five were among those executed afterwards by the British; O'Rahilly died bravely in a fire fight on the Friday of Easter Week.

In all that follows, it is important to remember that the IRB were only one element—although the most important and determined element—within MacNéill's Irish Volunteers. The rising was made in the name of the Volunteers but was actually the result of a secret IRB plot. The IRB itself was terribly enfeebled at the start of the war but a nationwide tour by Mac Diarmada arrested the decline by swearing in influential local Volunteer officers. Tom Clarke, meanwhile, was arguing for a rising while Britain was engrossed in the European war, a reprise of the old nationalist adage that 'England's difficulty is Ireland's opportunity'.

Small though its numbers were, the IRB now had key people in the councils of the Volunteers. Moreover, it had the ear of others who, although never members of the Brotherhood, were growing in influence. Pearse was the Volunteers' director of military organisation; Plunkett was director of military operations; MacDonagh was director of training and Ceannt was director of communications. None were members of the IRB, although all were sympathetic to the idea of a rising.

A complicated structure thus emerged in the run up to the rising. There was the formal body of the Irish Volunteers under the leadership of Eoin MacNéill whose purpose was frankly confused and unclear. Within its ranks, there were sworn members of the IRB, whose inner circle of Clarke, Mac Diarmada and Bulmer Hobson were planning a rising of some sort. They in turn had the ears of sympathisers like Pearse who, although not themselves in the IRB, were beginning to accept the necessity for a rising.

Out of this confusion, there emerged a military committee of three persons—Pearse, Plunkett and Ceannt—although what exactly they were a committee of was unclear, since they were affiliated neither to the Volunteers nor to the IRB. The difference was that whereas the leadership of the Volunteers was perfectly ignorant of the committee's existence, Tom Clarke was well aware of it. So it might be regarded as a kind of outwork of the IRB, in external association to it. This situation persisted until the committee was joined by Mac Diarmada, who had just served a prison term for a seditious speech. He promptly swore the other three into the IRB at last and renamed the body the military council.

In the meantime, Pearse had made his name. He was the son of an English monumental sculptor whose nationalism had been formed by his cultural concerns rather than by pure politics in the Fenian manner. He was an Irish-language enthusiast, journalist and teacher. His school, St Enda's in the southern suburbs of Dublin, was a hothouse of cultural nationalism, educationally progressive by the standards of the day, and financially precarious. He was a member of the Wolfe Tone club, an IRB front of which Clarke was president and Mac Diarmada vice-president. It was Clarke who asked Pearse, by now well known as a public speaker, to deliver the funeral oration at Glasnevin Cemetery, Dublin, over the coffin of Jeremiah O'Donovan Rossa. Rossa was an IRB veteran of the 1860s, imprisoned until 1871 and only released on condition that he left Ireland, which condition he fulfilled by going to America and helping to organise the dynamite war of the 1880s. By the time of his funeral, on 1 August 1915, he was an antique relic of earlier Fenian campaigns, but Pearse linked the generations in an oration of genuine brilliance, culminating with what is justly regarded as one of the finest perorations in Irish oratory:

Sean Mac Diarmada. (*Courtesy of the National Library of Ireland*)

'In a closer spiritual communion with him now than ever before or perhaps ever again, in a spiritual communion with those of his day, living and dead, who suffered with him in English prisons, in communion of spirit too with our own dear comrades who suffer in English prisons today, and speaking on their behalf as well as our own, we pledge to Ireland our love, and we pledge to English rule in Ireland our hate. This is a place of peace, sacred to the dead, where men should speak with all charity and with all restraint; but I hold it a Christian thing, as O'Donovan Rossa held it, to hate evil, to hate untruth, to hate oppression, and, hating them, to strive to overthrow them.

'Our foes are strong and wise and wary; but, strong and wise and wary as they are, they cannot undo the miracles of God who ripens in the hearts of young men the seeds sown by the young men of a former generation. And the seeds sown by the young men of '65 and '67 are coming to their miraculous ripening today. Rulers and Defenders of Realms had need to be wary if they would guard against such processes. Life springs from death; and from the graves of patriot men and women spring living nations. The Defenders of this Realm have worked well in secret and in the open. They think that they have pacified Ireland. They think that they have purchased half of us and intimidated the other half. They think that they have foreseen everything, think that they have provided against everything; but the fools, the fools, the fools!— they have left us our Fenian dead, and while Ireland holds these graves, Ireland unfree shall never be at peace.'

The plans that might give substance to Pearse's rhetoric proceeded apace. All those plotting the rising agreed on one essential: the necessity for German arms and aid, just as the United Irishmen in the 1790s had required the help of revolutionary France. That unhappy precedent—too little, too late—would later appear lavish in comparison with what would be forthcoming from the Reich.

Joseph Plunkett went to Berlin in June 1915 accompanied by Sir Roger Casement, one of the most exotic of the Irish nationalist leaders. He had been born in Ulster of a comfortable Protestant family. He joined the British colonial service and produced two reports which were major humanitarian documents, one detailing the horrific conditions under which native workers were maltreated in the Belgian Congo, the other a similar report on conditions among rubber plantation workers in South America. Knighted in 1911, he retired from the colonial service the following year. He had always been something of an outsider—his homosexuality might have played a part here in what was still an unenlightened age—and his attraction to Irish nationalism was certainly not blunted by his first-hand experience of colonialism at its worst in Africa and South America. He joined the Irish Volunteers in 1913.

Two years later, he found himself in Berlin with Plunkett. The latter had sketched out a rough plan for a rising with Pearse, uninhibited by the fact that neither of them had any military experience and were both men of letters rather than men of action. Plunkett was a journalist and poet of a mystic bent, the scion of a distinguished old Catholic family whose father was a papal count. He now tried to convince a clearly sceptical German government of the feasibility and practicality of a rising on Britain's domestic flank. The Germans remained non-committal.

Casement meanwhile stayed in Germany and tried to recruit an Irish Brigade from Irish prisoners of war, with scant success. He did, however, eventually secure 20,000 rifles and a million rounds of ammunition together with the means to ship them from Hamburg to Ireland in support of the rising.

The first concrete plans for the Easter Rising were laid at a meeting in Clontarf Town Hall in January 1916. It was decided that regardless of all other circumstances, a rising would take place in the coming April, on the symbolic occasion of Easter Sunday. Contact was made with Clan na Gael in New York. The labour leader James Connolly was co-opted onto the military council, lest his tiny Irish Citizen Army—a militia formed after the failure of the 1913 lockout in Dublin—embark on an abortive rebellion of their own. Incredibly, Connolly entertained the fantasy that his tiny force of barely 200 men could precipitate such a violent counter-reaction from the British that it would trip off an international socialist rebellion across Europe such as would end the war and destroy the ruling classes.

The plans advanced ever more secretly. By now, there was a division not just between the military council and the leadership of the Volunteers but between the council and the Supreme Council of the IRB itself, some of

A Volunteer mobilisation order for Easter Sunday 1916. (*Courtesy of the National Library of Ireland*) whose members—most notably Bulmer Hobson—were kept in the dark. Hobson was a known opponent of a futile rising, quoting the very constitution of the IRB itself in support of his view that a rising should only be attempted with clear public support and a reasonable prospect of success. The first condition was plainly absent and the second out of reach for want of German arms. The Casement shipment would be some help. It was on the high seas and was due to make landfall off Banna strand in County Kerry on Good Friday.

In the event, the landing was a fiasco which ended in the capture and then the scuttling of the *Aud*, the ship carrying the arms. Casement got ashore only to be arrested and to begin the final journey that would lead him to the scaffold in Pentonville.

Fearing that the influential Hobson would scupper their plans at the last minute, the military council kidnapped him and held him until the rising was safely under way. Not part of the heroic narrative, he was ignored in the later glorifications of the rising and forgotten by his countrymen.

MacNéill, the formal head of the Volunteers, knew that something odd was afoot but was unsure exactly what. He had previously dismissed any proposals for an early rising in a document of devastating clarity and logic, concluding that 'to my mind, those who feel impelled towards military action … are really impelled by a sense of feebleness or despondency or fatalism, or by an instinct of satisfying their own emotions or escaping from a difficult and complex situation'. In April

1916, he asked Pearse for reassurances that no insurrection was planned or imminent. Pearse gave him a bland assurance to that effect. Still not satisfied, he confronted Pearse again only to receive the devastating reply: 'We have used your name and influence for what they were worth, but we have done with you now. It is no use trying to stop us.'

––––

But try to stop it he did. MacNéill issued an order countermanding all Volunteer manoeuvres planned for Easter weekend, correctly seeing them as cover for the intended rising. Such manoeuvres had been a growing feature of Volunteer activity, especially in Dublin where every available man had paraded in military formation the previous St Patrick's Day.

Moreover, MacNéill despatched people who had cars to the provinces with countermanding orders. The O'Rahilly was the best known of these. He spent all of Saturday, day and night, driving around the midlands personally delivering the instruction that all previous orders for Easter Sunday 'are hereby rescinded, and no parades, marches or other movements of Irish Volunteers will take place'. MacNéill also ensured that the countermanding order was carried in the early editions of the *Sunday Independent.*

By now, on Easter Sunday morning, the troops mobilising for the rising were beginning to muster at

Liberty Hall. The Proclamation of the Republic was being printed nearby and all was in readiness. The effect of MacNéill's démarche was to leave the leaders of the rising in two minds: Clarke wanted to proceed immediately, or at least later on Sunday, on the sensible grounds that if they postponed to the Monday, even fewer men would mobilise. He was overruled. And so it was to be Easter Monday that would go down in Irish history.

In all this activity in the early months of 1916, what of the British authorities in Dublin Castle? The fabled seat of British rule, with its spy system and surveillance apparatus, had been a constant bulwark against every species of militant nationalism since the Act of Union.

Times had, however, changed. Asquith's Liberal government had espoused and passed the longed-for Home Rule Act and awaited the end of the war to hand over the domestic Irish administration to Redmond and his lieutenants. In such circumstances, a heavy-handed security policy along traditional coercive lines seemed inappropriate. Moreover, the chief secretary, Augustine Birrell, who had been in the job since 1907 (he was the longest serving of all chief secretaries), was neither of a confrontational nor an authoritarian temper. His under secretary—the head of the Irish civil service—Sir Matthew Nathan had come to the post as late as 1914 with no previous experience of Ireland and was, in many respects, still feeling his way. His previous postings had been in Sierra Leone, the Gold Coast (Ghana) and Hong Kong.

Eoin MacNéill. (*Courtesy of the National Library of Ireland*)

There were warnings from within the Irish administration of growing insurrectionary feeling. This was usually denominated as Sinn Féin activity, although it had absolutely nothing to do with that tiny and almost moribund party. Still, Sinn Féin became a generic for all advanced nationalism and the name stuck. Major Ivor Price, the Irish Command's intelligence officer, argued that the Irish Volunteers were a seditious organisation. This was regarded by Birrell as alarmist and exaggerated and perhaps only to be expected from a former senior RIC officer.

Birrell argued, not without reason, that to proscribe the Irish Volunteers while leaving the National Volunteers—and worse, the UVF—untouched made no sense. Birrell was a charming, witty, bookish man, a good literary critic and a dinner party favourite in London, where his *bon mots* were remembered. Temperamentally he was a liberal, reflexively averse to heavy-handed security measures. Nor was he a heavyweight at the cabinet table, where his brief seemed a distraction from the rather more important business of the war. He was the wrong man in the wrong place (or rather, not in the wrong place, for the most frequent complaint against him was that he spent far too much time in London and too little in Dublin). Given the weakening legitimacy of British government in Ireland, it is hard to see how policies such as those being urged by Major Price could have been carried through without playing totally into the radicals' hands.

Arthur Hamilton Norway was the head of the Irish postal service. He was aware of subversives in his service, for the post office was a favourite place of employment for IRB men and other advanced nationalists. Michael Collins was merely the best known of them, but in early 1916 they included such influential IRB figures as P.S. O'Hegarty. He too was struck by the apparently casual and relaxed view of the Castle. In a sense, the open parading and marching of the Volunteers in early 1916 acted as an unconscious bluff, lulling the authorities into the view that no actual conspiracy would declare itself so openly. It seemed to make sense to believe that the Volunteers were merely playing at soldiers.

The capture of Casement on Good Friday confirmed the authorities in their view that if something had been afoot, it was all scuppered now. It was a bank holiday weekend. Birrell, in London for a cabinet meeting, decided to stay there and make the most of the break. The army commander in Ireland, General Friend, left Dublin for London after hearing of the capture of Casement, assuming like so many others that that was that. The Irish Grand National would be run at Fairyhouse, north-west of Dublin, on Monday. That was to be the destination of choice for many officers and gentlemen. Dublin Castle would be left with fewer than thirty troops to guard it. It was off to the races.

03 | EASTER MONDAY

Arthur Hamilton Norway was a conscientious man. Although it was a bank holiday, he went to his office in the GPO to attend to some paper work. Shortly after 11.30, he got a telephone call from Sir Matthew Nathan in Dublin Castle, who asked him to come up to the Castle straight away. When he got there, he found Nathan closeted with Major Price. They were discussing the weekend's events in Kerry: the capture of Casement and the sinking of the *Aud*. They requested Norway, as head of the post office, to ensure that the postal and telegraph service in Munster be suspended except for military use.

Although fewer in number than hoped for, the various Volunteer musters gathered on that Monday morning and began to take up their pre-planned positions around the city. A group from the Citizen

Army occupied St Stephen's Green and, in a tactically naïve echo of the Western Front, dug themselves into trenches in the park. Volunteers under Thomas MacDonagh occupied the monumental Jacob's Biscuit factory in Bishop Street, the most impregnable of all positions. There were garrisons established at the Four Courts, with an outpost across the river at the Mendicity Institution; at the sprawling South Dublin Union; and at Boland's Mills in the south-east of the city centre, commanding the railway approach from the mail packet at Kingstown into Westland Row station. The officer commanding Boland's Mills was Eamon de Valera, destined to be the highest ranking Volunteer to survive the rising. He would be heard from again.

The main group assembled at Liberty Hall from 10 a.m. onwards and shortly before noon, under the command of James Connolly, marched out along Abbey Street heading for Sackville Street and their target, the General Post Office. A second group of Citizen Army men under the Abbey actor Sean Connolly (no relation of James) was sent off to try to invest Dublin Castle. A reserve was left behind in Liberty Hall to guard stores and reserve ammunition.

The reserve were soon startled to see a troop of the 5th & 12th Lancers coming up the quays. They were going to pass the very front door of Liberty Hall. They were escorting an ammunition convoy that had been landed at the North Wall. The men in Liberty Hall were under orders not to engage in any belligerent activity unless

Liberty Hall before the rising, with members of the Irish Citizen Army drawn up. (*Courtesy of the National Library of Ireland*)

attacked, so they had to suffer the frustration of letting the cavalrymen pass unmolested. They crossed the end of Sackville Street and debouched into Bachelors Walk, oblivious to the fact that James Connolly and his men, less than 200 yards distant, were about to trip off the most seismic event in modern Irish history.

Connolly's column turned into Sackville Street under the idle gaze of the citizenry who presumed that this was more toy soldier stuff. The column halted, whereupon Connolly barked out the command: 'Left turn—the GPO. Charge!'

Meanwhile, the 5th & 12th Lancers were trotting along the north quays towards the Four Courts, where the Volunteer garrison under the command of Edward Daly was busying itself constructing a barricade at the junction of Church Street and the quay.

The other Connolly, Sean, had now reached the Castle with his column of about thirty men and a few women auxiliaries. They were challenged by the member of the Dublin Metropolitan Police on routine duty. Connolly shot him dead. His name was James O'Brien. They then captured the six soldiers in the guard house, who were casually preparing lunch.

Price, Nathan and Norway, meeting nearby, heard the commotion and wondered what was going on. Price rushed out brandishing a revolver, saw that he was outnumbered and withdrew. Astonishingly, so did the insurgents. They cannot have been aware that they had captured the entire Castle garrison; even if the twenty-five or so men from the Ship Street Barracks adjacent had been deployed, the rebels would still have had a numerical advantage. It would have been impossible to hold the Castle for long with such a paltry force but the propaganda value of investing it would have been enormous.

But the whole plan of the rising did not envisage success in conventional military terms. No one was under any illusion about the outcome. James Connolly admitted candidly to his trade union colleague, William O'Brien: 'Bill, we are going out to be slaughtered.' The O'Rahilly, having returned to Dublin following his countermanding mission in the midlands, found that the rising was under way after all. He promptly joined the GPO garrison. He met Desmond Fitzgerald and admitted: 'They were determined to have a rising, so here we are.' Fitzgerald asked him: 'How long do you think that we can last?' 'By a miracle we might last for twenty-four hours,' O'Rahilly replied, 'but I don't think we'll go for that long.'

The knowledge that the rising was, *ab initio*, a gesture in arms rather than a full blown struggle to replace British rule in Ireland undoubtedly influenced much rebel thinking, none more so than Sean Connolly's when he failed to press home his advantage at the Castle. Instead he fell back on the nearby City Hall and the offices of the *Evening Mail* across on the far side of Dame Street. By 1.40 p.m., 180 relief troops had arrived at the Ship Street entrance to the Castle, out of sight and range of the rebels in the City Hall whose fate was now just a matter of time. Indeed, for the leader of the group, Sean Connolly, time was short indeed. Just after

2 p.m., while observing troop movements in the Castle from the domed roof of the City Hall, he took a stray bullet and died on the spot, watched by his fifteen-year-old brother.

The signal to all rebel positions that the rising was on was to be given by an explosion at the Magazine Fort in the Phoenix Park. A party of Volunteers forced an entrance but were unable to access the high explosive store, for the simple reason that the key was not in its appointed place: the officer in charge had it in his pocket at Fairyhouse races. Instead they had to make do with lesser explosives which duly went off but gave a report that was not even heard at the South Dublin Union, the nearest garrison as the crow flew. The commander of the Magazine Fort was serving in France, but his seventeen-year-old son tried to raise the alarm, sprinting towards the nearest phone to warn the authorities. Volunteer Gerry Holohan gave chase, caught up with him in a doorway just outside the Phoenix Park and shot the boy dead.

Meanwhile the Lancers continued towards the Four Courts. For the inexperienced Volunteers at the makeshift Church Street barricade, mounted Lancers were a formidable and frightening sight. As much from terror as from any other consideration, they fired at the cavalrymen. The effect was startling. Completely taken by surprise, the Lancers turned into a side street only to come under fire from other corners of the garrison adjacent. Two of their number died in the subsequent confusion.

Irish Volunteer Marches Cancelled

A SUDDEN ORDER.

The Easter manoeuvres of the Irish Volunteers, which were announced to begin to-day, and which were to have been taken part in by all the branches of the organisation in city and country, were unexpectedly cancelled last night.

The following is the announcement communicated to the Press last evening by the Staff of the Volunteers:—

April 22, 1915.

Owing to the very critical position, all orders given to Irish Volunteers for to-morrow, Easter Sunday, are hereby rescinded, and no parades, marches, or other movements of Irish Volunteers will take place. Each individual Volunteer will obey this order strictly in every particular.

EOIN MACNEILL

Eoin MacNéill's countermanding order. (*Courtesy of the National Library of Ireland*)

The main drama was being played out in the GPO. When Connolly and his men charged, they met no resistance from the nominal military guard at the door, for the very good reason that they had not been issued with any ammunition. The staff and customers were understandably perplexed and it took a while—and some unsubtle persuasion—to convince them that this was a serious business and that they all must leave.

With that, the Volunteers began fortifying the building. Windows were sandbagged, men ordered to their positions and Connolly—attended by his secretary, Winifred Carney—began dictating a stream of orders. Outposts were established across the street in department stores—principally Clery's, the leading store in the street—and in the Imperial Hotel. The hotel was the property of William Martin Murphy, the employer-villain of the 1913 lockout, and Connolly took malicious pleasure in having the Irish socialist flag, the starry plough, raised on its roof.

Two flags were raised aloft over the GPO. One was the green, white and orange tricolour, first seen in 1848 as an Irish analogue of the French republican *tricolore*. Just as the French flag used colour symbols—the Bourbon white embraced by the Parisian red and blue—so did the Irish. In this case, the white symbolised peace between the orange and green traditions, an aspiration that has, in the life of the flag, been honoured as much in the breach as in the observance.

The second flag, flown at the Princes Street corner of the building, was a creation by Countess Markievicz. This exotic, née Gore-Booth, was a daughter of the Anglo-Irish ascendancy and had been presented at court as a young woman in the 1880s. She then pursued a bohemian career as a painter in London and Paris, where she met her husband, a Polish-Ukrainian count. Returning to Ireland, she gradually embraced nationalist and labour causes and was a heroine of the 1913 lockout where she organised a soup kitchen in Liberty Hall. She was the founder of a number of republican youth organisations, most notably Na Fianna (roughly, the warriors), which became a kind of junior Volunteer movement. The flag she designed comprised the words Irish Republic on a green field. The material was rumoured to be part of an old bedspread. At all events, the sight of these three flags flying on either side of the capital's principal thoroughfare was one to stir the imagination.

All contemporary reports of what happened next tell of public apathy, the more remarkable in hindsight considering that what did happen was the central symbolic moment of the whole week. Patrick Pearse stepped out of the GPO and read the Proclamation of the Republic to an unresponsive audience.

The entrance to the Upper Castle Yard at Dublin Castle. (*Courtesy of the National Library of Ireland*)

POBLACHT NA H EIREANN

THE PROVISIONAL GOVERNMENT
OF THE
IRISH REPUBLIC
TO THE PEOPLE OF IRELAND

IRISHMEN AND IRISHWOMEN: In the name of God and of the dead generations from which she receives her old tradition of nationhood, Ireland, through us, summons her children to her flag and strikes for her freedom.

Having organised and trained her manhood through her secret revolutionary organisation, the Irish Republican Brotherhood, and through her open military organisations, the Irish Volunteers and the Irish Citizen Army, having patiently perfected her discipline, having resolutely waited for the right moment to reveal itself, she now seizes that moment, and, supported by her exiled children in America and by gallant allies in Europe, but relying in the first on her own strength, she strikes in full confidence of victory.

We declare the right of the people of Ireland to the ownership of Ireland, and to the unfettered control of Irish destinies, to be sovereign and indefeasible. The long usurpation of that right by a foreign people and government has not extinguished the right, nor can it ever be extinguished except by the destruction of the Irish people. In every generation the Irish people have asserted their right to national freedom and sovereignty; six times during the last three hundred years they have asserted it to arms. Standing on that fundamental right and again asserting it in arms in the face of the world, we hereby proclaim the Irish Republic as a Sovereign Independent State, and we pledge our lives and the lives of our comrades-in-arms to the cause of its freedom, of its welfare, and of its exaltation among the nations.

The Irish Republic is entitled to, and hereby claims, the allegiance of every Irishman and Irishwoman. The Republic guarantees religious and civil liberty, equal rights and equal opportunities to all its citizens, and declares its resolve to pursue the happiness and prosperity of the whole nation and all of its parts, cherishing all of the children of the nation equally and oblivious of the differences carefully fostered by an alien government, which have divided a minority from the majority in the past.

Until our arms have brought the opportune moment for the establishment of a permanent National, representative of the whole people of Ireland and elected by the suffrages of all her men and women, the Provisional Government, hereby constituted, will administer the civil and military affairs of the Republic in trust for the people.

We place the cause of the Irish Republic under the protection of the Most High God. Whose blessing we invoke upon our arms, and we pray that no one who serves that cause will dishonour it by cowardice, in humanity, or rapine. In this supreme hour the Irish nation must, by its valour and discipline and by the readiness of its children to sacrifice themselves for the common good, prove itself worthy of the august destiny to which it is called.

Signed on Behalf of the Provisional Government.
Thomas J. Clarke,
Sean Mac Diarmada, Thomas MacDonagh,
P. H. Pearse, Eamonn Ceannt,
James Connolly, Joseph Plunkett

Gradually crowds gathered in Sackville Street. There was some looting, as people from the nearby slums just off the north side of the street began to take advantage of the situation. A group of priests tried to move the growing crowd down the street towards O'Connell Bridge but it was a hopeless task: no sooner had they persuaded one group to move along than a larger one swelled in behind them. What eventually scattered the crowds was not priests but cavalry.

Dublin was very sparsely defended by the British. Not only was the Castle itself denuded of troops, there were no more than 400 regular troops distributed at the four principal barracks in the city. It was a troop of Lancers from Marlborough Barracks, on the edge of the Phoenix Park, which made its way to the top of Sackville Street by the Parnell Monument—the far end from O'Connell Bridge—and surveyed the scene. In the GPO, Connolly gave strict instruction that in the event of their charging

POBLACHT NA H EIREANN.
THE PROVISIONAL GOVERNMENT
OF THE
IRISH REPUBLIC
TO THE PEOPLE OF IRELAND.

IRISHMEN AND IRISHWOMEN : In the name of God and of the dead generations from which she receives her old tradition of nationhood, Ireland, through us, summons her children to her flag and strikes for her freedom.

Having organised and trained her manhood through her secret revolutionary organisation, the Irish Republican Brotherhood, and through her open military organisations, the Irish Volunteers and the Irish Citizen Army, having patiently perfected her discipline, having resolutely waited for the right moment to reveal itself, she now seizes that moment, and, supported by her exiled children in America and by gallant allies in Europe, but relying in the first on her own strength, she strikes in full confidence of victory.

We declare the right of the people of Ireland to the ownership of Ireland, and to the unfettered control of Irish destinies, to be sovereign and indefeasible. The long usurpation of that right by a foreign people and government has not extinguished the right, nor can it ever be extinguished except by the destruction of the Irish people. In every generation the Irish people have asserted their right to national freedom and sovereignty; six times during the past three hundred years they have asserted it in arms. Standing on that fundamental right and again asserting it in arms in the face of the world, we hereby proclaim the Irish Republic as a Sovereign Independent State, and we pledge our lives and the lives of our comrades-in-arms to the cause of its freedom, of its welfare, and of its exaltation among the nations.

The Irish Republic is entitled to, and hereby claims, the allegiance of every Irishman and Irishwoman. The Republic guarantees religious and civil liberty, equal rights and equal opportunities to all its citizens, and declares its resolve to pursue the happiness and prosperity of the whole nation and of all its parts, cherishing all the children of the nation equally, and oblivious of the differences carefully fostered by an alien government, which have divided a minority from the majority in the past.

Until our arms have brought the opportune moment for the establishment of a permanent National Government, representative of the whole people of Ireland and elected by the suffrages of all her men and women, the Provisional Government, hereby constituted, will administer the civil and military affairs of the Republic in trust for the people.

We place the cause of the Irish Republic under the protection of the Most High God, Whose blessing we invoke upon our arms, and we pray that no one who serves that cause will dishonour it by cowardice, inhumanity, or rapine. In this supreme hour the Irish nation must, by its valour and discipline and by the readiness of its children to sacrifice themselves for the common good, prove itself worthy of the august destiny to which it is called.

Signed on Behalf of the Provisional Government,

THOMAS J. CLARKE,
SEAN Mac DIARMADA,   THOMAS MacDONAGH,
P. H. PEARSE,   EAMONN CEANNT,
JAMES CONNOLLY.   JOSEPH PLUNKETT.

The Proclamation. (*Courtesy of the National Library of Ireland*) down the street no shots were to be fired until he barked out the order: he wanted them fully astride the building so that they could be caught fully broadside.

The Lancers came all right. Their commanding officer, Colonel Hammond, appears to have had a cavalryman's traditional belief in the intimidating power of mounted troops, especially on irregulars. They started down the street at a trot and eventually broke into a gallop with sabres drawn. Hammond's calculation may not have been wholly wrong, because Connolly's order was ignored and the GPO garrison began firing before the order was given. The result was three Lancers dead before they hit the ground and a fourth fatally wounded. Hammond sounded the retreat, leaving his casualties where they had fallen, and withdrew whence he had come.

In the words of W.J. Brennan-Whitmore, an eye-witness to the event and shortly to be placed in charge of the Volunteer position at the head of North Earl Street, across from the GPO: 'I cannot conceive anything more stupid than this sortie by mounted troops.'

———

The outlying garrisons saw little action on the Monday. While the GPO and the Four Courts had the satisfaction of their engagements with Lancers, and the City Hall group were now stoically awaiting their fate, which duly arrived overnight, the Stephen's Green detachment, under the less than confident leadership of Michael Mallin, was unaccountably digging trenches for itself. Its reward was to get drenched, for it rained heavily on Monday night—the only exception all week to the fabled rebellion weather. No attempt was made to take over the Shelbourne Hotel, the tallest building in the area. Instead, Mallin's second-in-command, Countess Markievicz, enthralled the guests in the Shelbourne Hotel by prancing up and down along the north side of the Green in plain view and in full uniform. The garrison achieved nothing more heroic than killing an unarmed policeman and an elderly actor who was attempting to recover his property which had been commandeered for a rebel barricade.

Just as no attempt was made to capture the Shelbourne, neither was any assault made on Trinity College, strategically the most important position in the city. It was defended only by its Officer Training Corps (OTC) who would have been useless against a determined attack. More to the point, it would have given access to the OTC's arms and ammunition store, which would have augmented the Volunteers' scarce resources of materiel.

The first of the other principal garrisons were at Jacob's factory in the south inner city, commanding the crossing of the Grand Canal from Portobello Barracks in Rathmines. It was impregnable to attack from anything other than the heaviest artillery but equally its uselessness as an offensive possibility was underscored by its minimal contribution to the events of the week. It was the last garrison to surrender, not because of heroism but because of its remoteness from all that went on around it. It was the last garrison to get the news of the general surrender. Although geographically close to the action, it assumed the status of a medieval donjon wherein its troops were safely sequestered from the tumult without.

It missed an opportunity to inflict real damage on a party of troops from Portobello Barracks heading to the relief of Dublin Castle when—just as with the Lancers in Sackville Street—the inexperienced Volunteers fired prematurely in defiance of MacDonagh's orders. The military, alerted to the danger, withdrew and rerouted.

The second major garrison was Eamonn Ceannt's command at the South Dublin Union. This sprawling 52-acre site was in the south-west of the city and the idea of investing it was to harass any British troops being sent in as reinforcements via the nearby Kingsbridge station, the disembarkation point for troops from the Curragh Camp. Any troops marching along the quays, on either side of the river, towards the Four Courts on the north side or its outpost at the Mendicity Institution on the south side, could be harassed. But given the paltry numbers that actually mustered and the difficulty of securing their base in the SDU with such scant resources, the garrison was nearly useless as an offensive force. Indeed, one is again struck by the essentially defensive disposition of all garrisons, based on an overall battle plan that did not actually envisage military success but a symbolic gesture in arms.

Men of the GPO garrison. (*Kilmainham Gaol Collection*)

None the less, snipers from the garrison were able to mount an ambush on troops marching towards Thomas Street. This prompted a furious British response that resulted in an encircling counter-attack on the SDU itself, where weight of numbers quickly told. Ceannt's men fought all day with real courage as their garrison space shrank all the time.

The other major garrison was at Boland's Mills and its strategic aim was similar to that at the South Dublin Union. The mills, a formidable Victorian industrial structure approaching if not quite matching the scale of Jacob's, commanded the railway line from the south-east and specifically from Kingstown where any reinforcements sent from Britain would disembark. Again it was an essentially defensive disposition. But it was, none the less, to produce the best offensive performance by the rebels in the entire course of Easter Week.

First of all, the position gave direct access to the railway itself, unlike the SDU. The garrison troops busied themselves by taking over the terminal at Westland Row—not without some farcical scenes—and, more to the point, by digging up the track on the approach. Incoming trains could now proceed no closer to the city than the suburban station at Lansdowne Road. It meant that any troops inbound would have to march in by road, almost certainly along Northumberland Road where they would cross the canal at Mount Street Bridge. With this in mind, the garrison sent a small force to occupy the tall houses that commanded the approach to the bridge. In addition, the Boland's Mills garrison was expected to 'dominate' the army barracks at Beggar's Bush, which lay under the railway embankment that ran between Lansdowne Road and Westland Row stations. In fact, they could have invested it had they but known that it was completely undefended.

It would have been of little use to them for, like the garrison at the South Dublin Union, de Valera's men were too few in number to command the large area they were nominally assigned. The manner in which they concentrated their resources at strategic pressure points brought the rebel forces the greatest success of the week.

04 | TUESDAY

Thomas MacDonagh's garrison in Jacob's had originally been due to deploy between Clontarf and Amiens Street station—the terminal from Belfast—on the same logic as de Valera's garrison across the river at Beggar's Bush: to prevent and disrupt the arrival of crown reinforcements. But lack of numbers and muddle conspired against them and they redeployed to Jacob's, leaving the line into the station available and the north-east approaches to the city centre empty of rebels. The first reinforcements duly arrived there the following morning.

However, the more significant arrivals were at Kingsbridge station in the south-west. Here troops arrived during the night from the Curragh, about thirty-five miles away, under the command of Brigadier-General W.H.M. Lowe. By morning, they began to take up their positions. Lowe's plan was to throw a cordon around the city centre, within which the GPO and Four Courts garrisons would be trapped and isolated from outlying garrisons. This plan worked more or less as conceived, although the original southern base of the cordon had to be moved away from the south quays to Thomas Street because the troops came under heavy fire from the small Four Courts outpost at the Mendicity Institution. Likewise, on the north side, they had to deploy away from North King Street because of the proximity of the actual Four Courts rebels.

None the less, the British army had, by Tuesday evening, successfully embraced the city centre in a cordon that ran clockwise from Kingsbridge to Blackhall Place to North Brunswick Street, by Broadstone station and Parnell Street, Gardiner Street, Tara Street, College Green, Dame Street, Christ Church and Thomas Street. In addition, troops had slipped in the side door of the Shelbourne Hotel in the small hours of Tuesday morning and had managed to get a number of Vickers machine guns up to the fourth floor. They had a clear field of fire into the sodden trenches in St Stephen's Green.

Five rebels died. The rest, about 100 in all, fled to the relative safety of the Royal College of Surgeons on the west side of the Green. It was the most imposing building on that side, although still much smaller than the Shelbourne.

There was little action in Sackville Street on the Tuesday but the breakdown of law and order presented a priceless opportunity for people from the nearby slums to loot the

Mount Street Bridge. (*Courtesy of the National Library of Ireland*)

undefended shops. It placed Connolly in a moral quandary. These were his people, the poorest of the poor from some of the most awful slums in Europe, but they were both disgracing the rising and hindering its progress. Mac Diarmada was sent out to remonstrate with them, to no avail. Francis Sheehy-Skeffington, perhaps the best-known eccentric in Dublin (an honour subject to intense competition at any moment in history), also tried in vain. 'Skeffy' was a pacifist, a feminist and a vegetarian given to wearing home-spun tweeds in the Shavian manner. Connolly was reduced to firing over the heads of the crowd and sending a party under Sean T. O'Kelly to mount a guard on the shops.

The situation on the far side of the street from the GPO stabilised somewhat when Brennan-Whitmore was sent across by Connolly to invest various premises in the hope of holding off any reinforcements coming up from Amiens Street station either by Talbot Street/North Earl Street or by Abbey Street. His men constructed a barricade across the top of North Earl Street where it gave way into Sackville Street. Brennan-Whitmore was lucky in that one of his men somehow got hold of a long coil of wire which was used to interlace and strengthen the otherwise rickety barricade. Pearse and Connolly both came across separately from the GPO and declared the barricade flimsy until Brennan-Whitmore invited each in turn to try and disturb it. Braced by the wire, it held. Brennan-Whitmore admired Connolly, whom he described as 'always sharp and decisive'. He was less obviously admiring of Pearse whose 'mind was obviously up in the clouds' but he acknowledged that Pearse 'was not just respected by the little garrison, he was almost worshipped'.

It was Pearse, the rhetorician and propagandist, who issued the first—and only—edition of *Irish War News* at 9.30 a.m. on Tuesday. Propaganda of the deed was now followed by propaganda of the word. If the rising was a poets' rebellion, as was frequently stated later, the literary appeal to public sentiment was a logical corollary of the whole enterprise. It was also firmly in the tradition of European nineteenth-century rev-olutionary and insurrectionary endeavour. Pearse here stood with Lamartine, Herzen and Wagner—all veterans of 1848—as much as with his apostolic succession of Irish resistance: 1798, the Young Irelanders, the Fenians and so on. Even the manner of the urban revolt itself was reminiscent of the European past: the barricades, the public buildings invested, the expectation of counter-attack from the forces of the old regime. It might have been Paris or Dresden in 1848. It was a lesson not lost on Michael Collins, a twenty-five-year-old Corkman in the GPO. When he came to direct the next phase of republican resistance to British rule in Ireland a few years later, he used methods remote from those of the romantic revolutions and well adapted both to Irish and twentieth-century circumstances.

Pearse's single-issue news sheet may have had a butterfly life but it made its point, albeit with some pardonable exaggeration, and established a narrative that long outlived its author and the rising itself.

O'Connell Bridge and environs before and after the rising. (*Courtesy of the National Library of Ireland*)

April 25th 1916

Irish War News
The Irish Republic

Vol. 1, No. 1, Dublin, Tuesday April 25th, 1916.
Price One Penny.
Stop Press!
The Irish Republic

Irish War News is published today because a momentous thing has happened. The Irish Republic has been proclaimed in Dublin, and a Provisional Government has been appointed to administer its affairs.

• The following has been named as the Provisional Government:

Thomas J. Clarke,
Sean Mac Diarmada,
P. H. Pearse,
James Connolly,
Thomas MacDonagh,
Eamonn Ceannt,
Joseph Plunkett.

The Irish Republic was proclaimed by poster which was prominently displayed in Dublin.

At 9.30 a.m. this morning the following statement was made by Commandant-General P. H. Pearse:

The Irish Republic was proclaimed in Dublin on Easter Monday, April 24, at 12 noon. Simultaneously with the issue of the proclamation of the Provisional Government the Dublin Division of the Army of the Republic, including the Irish Volunteers, the Citizen Army, Hibernian Rifles, and other bodies occupied dominating positions in the city. The GPO was seized at 12 noon, the Castle attacked at the same moment, and shortly afterwards the Four Courts were occupied. The Irish troops hold the City Hall and dominate the Castle. Attacks were immediately commenced by the British forces, and everywhere were repulsed.

At the moment of writing this report (9.30 a.m., Tuesday) the Republican forces hold their positions and the British forces have nowhere broken through. There has been heavy and continuous fighting for nearly 24 hours, the casualties of the enemy have been much more numerous than those on the Republican side. The Republican forces everywhere are fighting with splendid gallantry. The populace of Dublin are plainly with the Republic, and the officers and men are everywhere cheered as they march through the city. The whole centre of the city is in the hands of the Republic, whose flag flies from the GPO.

Commandant-General P. H. Pearse is Commandant in Chief of the Army of the Republic and is President of the Provisional Government. Commandant-General James Connolly is commanding Dublin districts.

Communication with the country is largely cut, but reports to hand show that the country is rising.

Bodies of men from Kildare and Fingal have already reported in Dublin.

Later in the day, Pearse issued a 'Manifesto to the Citizens of Dublin' which he read out from the foot of Nelson Pillar.

'The Republican forces hold the lines taken up at 12 noon on Easter Monday and nowhere, despite fierce and almost continuous attacks of the British troops, have the lines been broken through. The country is rising in answer to Dublin's call and the final achievement of Ireland's freedom is now, with God's help, only a matter of days. The valour, self-sacrifice and discipline of Irish men and women are about to win for our country a glorious place among the nations.... The British troops have been firing on our women and on our Red Cross. On the other hand, Irish Regiments in the British army have refused to act against their fellow-countrymen.'

The country was not rising. There were no mobilisations of any significance outside Dublin. The scattered garrisons around the city, of which two were trapped within the British cordon, were on their own.

Yet Pearse's fictions were to have the last word. Out of this hopeless military position, a foundation myth was born.

Lower O'Connell Street after the rising. (© *RTÉ Stills Library*)

It had been an article of faith for James Connolly that the British would not use artillery against rebel positions. In this, as with other big considerations, this intelligent, practical and attractive man showed a dismaying naïveté. Connolly was a socialist in the heroic age of socialism, an age in which to many the ravages of the industrial revolution seemed disproportionate to its achievements. Moreover, it had created an immisserated urban proletariat whose cause became that of socialists everywhere. Bad as the condition of the lower working class was in industrial cities, it was worse again in older cities like Dublin or Naples that had been little touched by nineteenth-century industry. Connolly's socialism was a perfectly rational response to the hideous conditions prevailing in early twentieth-century Dublin. Unfortunately, it led him into ideological blind alleys. Not the least of these concerned the relationship between economic and military power.

Connolly argued that no capitalist government would deploy artillery and thus destroy private property within its own borders. He seemed strangely ignorant of the Paris Commune. At any rate, his illusions were shattered in the middle of Tuesday afternoon when an 18-pound field gun, recently arrived by train from Athlone and set up in the grounds of Grangegorman hospital in the north-west of the city, scattered an outlying rebel barricade in the suburb of Phibsborough. It was a portent of bigger things to come.

Out beyond Phibsborough and Grangegorman, at the western end of the North Circular Road, lay the Phoenix

Park. In the middle of the park stood the Viceregal Lodge, a house originally built as a residence for the park ranger in the eighteenth century and later extended by Francis Johnston—ironically, the architect of the GPO wherein the forces of the republic were now established—when it became the official seat of the Viceroy (or Lord Lieutenant) of Ireland. The Viceroy was the representative of the crown in Ireland, just as Birrell the chief secretary was the representative of the government. The presiding Viceroy, only recently appointed, was Ivor Churchill Guest, otherwise Lord Wimborne.

Wimborne had not been impressed by the response of either Birrell or of Sir Matthew Nathan, the under secretary, to the alarums of the previous week. The rumours of rebel mobilisation and the Kerry landings had seemed to him causes for genuine concern and he had urged stern preventative measures on Birrell and Nathan. They temporised, arguing that precipitate arrests of suspects would be illegal. In this they were almost certainly correct. But now Wimborne could at least reflect that he had been right and they had been wrong. The thing was: what to do? He was concerned for the safety of his family, isolated as they were in the middle of the same park where the murders of Burke and Cavendish in 1882 were still in living memory. The Dublin Metropolitan Police had been withdrawn to barracks after losing three men to the rebels on the Monday. The civil government in the Castle was in disarray.

Wimborne declared martial law in Dublin. Whether he had the authority to do this without consulting the political and legal arms of government was moot. He was, after all, merely the ornamental and ceremonial representative of the crown in Ireland. In normal circumstances, any such declaration would require his official signature but it is doubtful if he had the authority to initiate such a decree on his own initiative. That said, the point was academic in the circumstances because of the impotence of the civil government and the communication gap. Birrell was still in England and did not return to Ireland until Wednesday.

Martial law had not been declared in Ireland since the aftermath of the 1798 rising. It was offensive to English sensibility, smacking of Prussian militarism and army rule. It was one thing to employ it in the farther corners of the empire, which perforce required a strong military presence to ensure law and order. It was quite something else to declare it in the heart of the metropolitan United Kingdom. Birrell, good liberal to the end, was horrified by Wimborne's action and tried to ensure that at least martial law would be confined to the city. But Birrell was a busted flush politically and so was Asquith's Liberal Party. The British war cabinet, in the middle of a European war that was going badly, was in ever growing hock to the military, upon whom the life of the nation now depended. The military knew what was wrong with Ireland. Kid glove liberals like Birrell were to blame. It was time for the smack of firm government. Martial law was extended to all Ireland until further notice.

It was soon to result in muddle and tragedy. Francis Sheehy-Skeffington had spent part of the day

In order to prevent the further slaughter of Dublin
citizens, and in the hope of saving the lives of our
followers now surrounded and hopelessly outnumbered, the
members of the Provisional Government present at Head-
Quarters have agreed to an unconditional surrender, and the
Commandants of the various districts in the City and Country
will order their commands to lay down arms.

P. H. Pearse

29th April 1916

3.45 p.m.

I agree to these conditions for the men only
under my own Command in the Moore
Street District and for the men in
the Stephen's Green Command.

James Connolly

April 29/16

On consultation with Commandant Ceannt
and other officers I have decided to
agree to unconditional surrender also.

Thomas MacDonagh.

The Surrender of Headquarters.

The surrender document. (*Courtesy of the National Library of Ireland*) trying to establish a citizen volunteer group to deter looting, in pursuit of which aim he had called a public meeting for Tuesday evening. Before going to the meeting, he intended to go home to his house in Rathmines to check that all was well with his wife and small son. He was attended by a small gaggle of people: as a well-known eccentric and campaigner, he was used to this. His route took him over Portobello Bridge, beside which stood Davy's public house.

A small detachment of troops from the nearby Portobello Barracks had invested Davy's in order to command the canal bridge. They had been given a bad time of it in the previous twenty-four hours by MacDonagh's men in Jacob's, which loomed over their position. They were tired, nervous and exposed. The officer in charge at Davy's regarded the small retinue attending Sheehy-Skeffington as a breach of martial law. He was arrested and led to the nearby barracks. He was detained without charge.

Later that night, Sheehy-Skeffington was hauled out of the guard room by Captain J.C. Bowen-Colthurst, an experienced officer and a veteran of the retreat from Mons in 1914. Bowen-Colthurst had taken it into his head, for reasons as obscure now as then, to lead a raiding party along Harcourt Road to the shop of Alderman James Kelly. This was probably a case of mistaken identity, for this Kelly was a Protestant and a Unionist. Bowen-Colthurst may have confused him with Alderman Tom Kelly, a Catholic and a member of Sinn Féin. The raiding party comprised Bowen-Colthurst, a junior officer, Lieutenant Wilson, and forty men. Sheehy-Skeffington was to come along as a hostage. Bowen-Colthurst ordered the pacifist to say his prayers and when Skeffy refused—he was an atheist along with everything else—Bowen-Colthurst intoned the following words over him: 'O Lord God, if it should please Thee to take away the life of this man, forgive him for Our Lord Jesus Christ's sake.'

On Rathmines Road, the raiding party came upon two youths, Lawrence Byrne and J.J. Coade. Bowen-Colthurst, clearly agitated, roared at them that martial law was in force and that he could shoot them 'like dogs'. Which is precisely what he then proceeded to do to Coade. Leading his men, with poor Sheehy-Skeffington in tow, he continued to Portobello Bridge, where he left Wilson with the hostage and instructions to shoot him if the raid went wrong or the position otherwise came under fire.

Alderman Kelly was not at home. Nothing daunted, the raiding party chucked in a hand grenade and went on to wreck the place. They found two perfectly innocent men there and arrested them. They were both journalists, Thomas Dickson, a disabled Scot, and Patrick MacIntyre. They then returned to the barracks with this pair, collecting Sheehy-Skeffington along the way, and incarcerated all three. It was now after midnight, the early hours of Wednesday morning.

05 | WEDNESDAY

The *Helga* was a 323-ton, 156-foot fisheries protection vessel. She had been built in 1908 in the Liffey Dockyard. When the Great War broke out, she was deployed on anti-submarine patrols. On the outbreak of the rising, she was instructed to sail around from Kingstown and into the mouth of the Liffey. This she did on Tuesday afternoon, stopping only to fire a few three-inch shells into the rear of de Valera's position at Boland's Mills. Dev's response was clever: he ran a republican tricolour up aloft over the empty Ringsend Distillery adjacent, thus diverting the *Helga*'s fire from his own position. In all she discharged sixteen rounds, most of them into the distillery.

By Tuesday evening, the *Helga* was moored along the wall at the city end of Sir John Rogerson's Quay. On the far quay lay the Custom House and bridging the river beyond it was the hideous Loop Line Bridge, a trellised metal structure built in 1891 to link the railway termini of Westland Row and Amiens Street. Beyond the Loop Line, on the same side as the Custom House, Liberty Hall stood at the east end of Eden Quay.

Liberty Hall faced across Butt Bridge—a road bridge beside the Loop Line—and had a clear view along Tara Street on the south side along to the side wall of Trinity College, which enclosed the view. Early on Wednesday morning, 'workmen' were allegedly digging up parts of Tara Street to deal with some problems with the drains. In reality, they were members of the Officer Training Corps from Trinity, who had been relieved the previous evening by a detachment of the regular army that had entered the city under Lowe's command. They weren't digging drains. Rather they were digging out emplacements for two 18-pound artillery pieces that the army intended to deploy against Liberty Hall.

Precisely at 8 a.m. the assault on Liberty Hall began. The *Helga* fired a shell that careered into the Loop Line Bridge, making a metallic clang that was heard all over the city. The crew adjusted their sights and fired again, and this time the shell described an arc that carried it across the bridges and hit Liberty Hall. Meanwhile, the 18-pounders in Tara Street opened up for good measure. In no time, Liberty Hall was a shell.

It was a lot of trouble to take over a building that was empty save for its caretaker. This man, Peter Ennis by name, very sensibly ran out onto Eden Quay where he

Countess Markievicz (marked with an X) among the Volunteer prisoners after the rising. (© *RTÉ Stills Library*)

became a target for army snipers. A reporter watched him literally run for his life:

'A machine gun is turned on him. Bullets hit the pavement in front of him and behind him, they strike the roadway and the walls of the building along his route and still he runs on and on. I hold my breath in awe as I watch his mad career. Will he escape? He will … he won't. "My God!" I exclaim as a bullet raises a spark from the pavement right at his toe. A hundred yards in nine seconds—a record! Nonsense, this man does the distance in five and disappears, his breath in his fist, his heart in his mouth but—safe!'

The assault on Liberty Hall was farce, prompted either by false intelligence as to its military significance or by its symbolic value. What happened next was tragedy.

Across the city, in Portobello Barracks, Captain J.C. Bowen-Colthurst had not slept much the previous night. According to his later testimony, he had pored over documents taken from Alderman Kelly's shop following the raid and over other papers found on Frank Sheehy-Skeffington's person. At 9 a.m. on Wednesday morning, he led Skeffington and the other two prisoners from the guardroom, informing the officer in charge that he was 'taking these prisoners out and I am going to shoot them as I think that it is the right thing to do'.

He proceeded to do so, forming an ad hoc firing squad of seven to dispatch Skeffington, Dickson and McIntyre. It was a tragic irony. Skeffington, the best-known pacifist in Ireland, who had spent most of the previous day trying to stop looting and to start an anti-looting watch group (an endearingly typical and quixotic initiative in the circumstances) met his death before a firing squad. He was one who could only have been considered a danger to the public by a madman, which is what Bowen-Colthurst was. Even then, Bowen-Colthurst was not relieved of his duties and he went on to kill at least two more innocents in cold blood before a stop was put to his progress. He would have got away with his crimes were it not for the courage of a single fellow-officer whose subsequent efforts—few if any of them welcomed by his brother officers—eventually led to Bowen-Colthurst's court-martial. He was found guilty but insane and was committed to Broadmoor. After a short spell there, he was removed to a hospital in Canada. Less than two years after his conviction, he was deemed cured and was released. He retired from the army at forty, was granted a pension and lived to be almost ninety. Major Sir Francis Vane, the officer whose efforts led to his conviction, was rewarded with a dishonourable discharge.

———

The 18-pounder guns used so superfluously against Liberty Hall were soon at work nearby. Later that morning, artillery launched the assault on the GPO garrison and the gradual destruction of Lower Sackville

Joseph M. Plunkett. (*Courtesy of the National Library of Ireland*)

Street began. Connolly had believed that no capitalist government would wilfully destroy private property. Now he could see it coming to pass before his eyes.

Up along the river, Sean Heuston's tiny garrison at the Mendicity Institution on Usher's Quay was tying down army reinforcements marching up from Kingsbridge station, as well as providing some cover for the larger Four Courts garrison on the north side. James Connolly had not envisaged this outpost as being anything more than a temporary thing, designed to harry troops from barracks in the south-west of the city while the Four Courts garrison over the way was entrenching itself. Accordingly, it had been starved of rations and ammunition, since no one had expected it to be still functioning on the third day of the rising. Heuston's men were outnumbered by more than ten to one. None the less, they inflicted over a hundred casualties on the British before they were eventually surrounded. Had they beaten a tactical retreat the previous day, they would probably have got away and been able to rejoin the Four Courts garrison. But by Wednesday they had made such a thorough nuisance of themselves that the army was determined to root them out. Moreover, by investing the rising ground up towards Thomas Street, to the rear of Heuston's position, they had a clear field of fire.

The final assault began at noon and lasted an hour before Heuston hung out a white flag and the Mendicity became the first rebel position in the city to surrender.

The afternoon brought better fortune for the Volunteers, indeed their greatest single success of the week. A small detachment of men from the Boland's Mills garrison had been sent to occupy Clanwilliam House at Mount Street Bridge. This tall, late Georgian building, four storeys over basement, commanded the approach to the canal bridge along Northumberland Road. An even smaller group invested 25 Northumberland Road.

Troop reinforcements had been arriving all night in Kingstown. Many believed that they had been despatched to France and were startled to discover that they were in Ireland. It was decided that they should march towards their destinations in two columns. The Derbyshire troops were to take the inland route via Donnybrook to their destination, the Royal Hospital in Kilmainham, just west of the city centre near Kingsbridge station, which they reached safely. The Nottinghamshire troops appeared to be bound for Trinity College and marched via the suburb of Ballsbridge and along Northumberland Road, which brought them straight towards Mount Street Bridge.

The garrison in Clanwilliam House was tiny, a mere seven men, with a further five in 25 Northumberland Road and in a nearby school. The first volley was fired from no. 25 and accounted for ten men of the Sherwood Foresters. The inexperienced troops took time to regroup and identify the sources of enemy fire. A series of direct advances on the bridge itself were met with withering fire from the tiny group in Clanwilliam House.

The battle raged all afternoon and into the evening. The house at 25 Northumberland Road was not cleared out until 5 p.m.: one of the two Volunteers, Michael Malone, was killed but the other, Seumas Grace, escaped. It took until 8 p.m. to take the school. By nightfall, sheer weight of numbers told. Clanwilliam House was an inferno and was finally evacuated. The Volunteers had lost eight of their twelve men; the British had 230 dead or wounded.

———

This extraordinary success for the rebels in the south-east approaches to the city could not disguise what was happening in the centre. With the Mendicity Institution knocked out of play, the army noose tightened ever more around the Four Courts. As much to boost morale as anything, the garrison commander, Edward Daly, ordered an attack on the nearby Linenhall Barracks. It was defended, if that is the term, by its only residents: forty unarmed members of the Army Pay Corps. The Four Courts party duly captured the barracks but did not have the men to garrison it. So later in the day, they torched it rather than have it recaptured by the British. It would have been fatal to have allowed regular troops to invest a position so close to the Four Courts itself. The fire was enormous, destroying not only the barracks but many nearby tenements. The smoke could be seen all over the city and Daly was sufficiently alarmed that he feared the conflagration could engulf the entire city centre. Naturally, given the circumstances, the city fire brigade did not turn out.

The shell that was Liberty Hall. (© *RTÉ Stills Library*)

As it was, things were getting hotter all the time for the city centre rebel garrisons. The British had established firing positions in high buildings on both sides of the river: the Bermingham Tower in Dublin Castle; Guinness's brewery; Christ Church cathedral; Jervis Street hospital; Broadstone station. From these positions, they kept up a constant and relentless fire on rebel positions.

At 9 p.m. on Wednesday, the government announced the appointment of Sir John Grenfell Maxwell as the supreme military commander of British forces in Ireland. His instructions were 'to take all such measures as may in his opinion be necessary for the prompt suppression of insurrection in Ireland and may be accorded a free hand in regard to the movement of all troops now in Ireland or which may be placed under his command hereafter and also in regard to such measures as may seem to him advisable…'

The vice was closing. Militarily, the rising was a failure by Wednesday night. Brennan-Whitmore, still ensconced in his sub-garrison on the north side of Sackville Street across from the GPO, reckoned that there was little point in fighting on in the prevailing circumstances, sitting ducks for the final counter-attack. His favoured policy was to retreat through the back streets to the countryside and there to regroup for a guerrilla campaign.

There were, however, practical problems in the way of this. On his side of the street, any such retreat—even had it been sanctioned by Connolly, which it had not—

would have been through Dublin's worst tenements. Here lived many 'remittance women' whose husbands were serving on the Western Front and who regarded the rebels as dreamy middle-class fools, or worse. Moreover, many of the women were widows of men killed at the first battle of Ypres a year earlier and the coincidence of the anniversary and the outbreak of the rising did little to lessen their hostility. With no sure guide through the back streets, and with the north-east of the city—to which any successful retreat, however improbable, would have carried them—securely in government hands, all such thought was fantasy.

Yet Brennan-Whitmore was on to something. And across the street in the GPO, a twenty-five-year-old Volunteer from West Cork was thinking similar thoughts, which he would have the opportunity to act on in due course. His name was Michael Collins.

But for the moment they were trapped. There was no plan B, no line of retreat prepared nor any alternative plan of battle. The rising was theatre and gesture, not really war at all. It was symbolic statement written in blood. So, for the moment, as Wednesday passed into Thursday, there was nothing for it but to sit tight and see what the morrow would bring.

06 | THURSDAY

The morrow brought fire. The British relentlessly tightened their cordon around the city centre and increased their artillery attacks. The lower part of Sackville Street was in flames by day's end. The heat from the nearby fires made the GPO position almost untenable and only the hosing down of the sacking on the barricaded windows saved the garrison from evacuation.

At 10 p.m., after twelve hours of relentless bombardment, an oil works opposite the GPO caught fire, making a dangerous situation truly desperate. A series of dramatic explosions set sparks showering onto the roof of the GPO.

The city's economy was near collapse. There were food shortages, as normal supplies could not get in. Shops closed. All classes suffered, but as always in these circumstances, the poor suffered most. There was genuine hunger in the city.

The fighting went on. At the South Dublin Union, Eamonn Ceannt still had over 100 men at his disposal. They were under ceaseless attack from the British. It was close fighting, with both sides tunnelling through walls to advance or retreat—and all this going on in a medical facility with more than 3,000 terrified and indigent patients and the staff who were committed to caring for them. For the Volunteers, the real hero was Ceannt's second-in-command, Cathal Brugha.

Brugha had been born Charles William St John Burgess in 1874 of mixed English and Irish parentage. His father was a businessman of sufficient means to be able to have his son educated by the Jesuits at Belvedere, then even more than now an elite private school for the children of the Catholic middle class. He was therefore firmly in a tradition which also embraced other republican leaders: de Valera, Thomas MacDonagh and Pearse had all been privately educated and had been among the tiny minority of Irish Catholics who had received a university education. Young Burgess did not get that far, for his father's business failed and he was withdrawn from Belvedere at the age of sixteen and launched on the world of work. By the time he was thirty-five, he was co-founder of a Dublin business house that survives to this day. He was in most regards a conventional success.

Charles Burgess had long since become Cathal Brugha. Like so many of his generation, the Gaelic League had made a profound impression on him. He

James Connolly

JAMES CONNOLLY (1868-1916) born in Edinburgh of a Co. Monaghan father, was Commandant-General of the Dublin Division. He was a member of the Military Council and Provisional Government. He founded the Irish Socialist Republican Party in Dublin in 1896. In 1903 he emigrated to the U.S.A., but returned after seven years. With Padraic Pearse he led the main Insurgent force from Liberty Hall to the G.P.O. Severely wounded during the fighting, he was taken after the surrender to Dublin Castle. Despite his condition he was executed—sitting on a chair—on May 12th, in Kilmainham Jail.

Printed in the Republic of Ireland by DAOL, Cork

James Connolly. (*National Archive*)

had joined it in 1899, in his mid-twenties, and thereafter was a cultural nationalist. He was a founding member of the Irish Volunteers in 1913 and was appointed a lieutenant in the new body. A natural radical, he followed the most advanced nationalist positions and thus found himself a prominent figure in the rising. As second-in-command in the South Dublin Union, he was acknowledged as having rallied the Volunteers at a time when they might otherwise have thrown in the towel; his determination and example certainly extended the garrison's resistance.

Brugha paid a personal price for his courage. In defending one of the barricades, he suffered multiple wounds that left him disabled for the rest of his life. He survived the rising and went on to become chief of staff of the IRA from 1917 to 1919; he fought in the War of Independence, took the anti-Treaty side in 1922 and died almost literally in a blaze of glory in O'Connell Street (as Sackville Street had then become) in the Civil War, charging suicidally from a burning building when all was lost.

In one sense, Brugha was typical of nothing or no one but himself. But in another, he was very typical indeed. Middle class, educated, energetic and intelligent, entranced by a cultural and revolutionary myth, a radical unhappy with the accommodating bourgeois world that bred him, he was representative not just of the radicals who made the revolution in Ireland but also of that greater weariness with the late Victorian world that informed many of his generation in Europe.

His heroics at the South Dublin Union ensured that the little garrison was never overrun, despite the ferocious close-quarters nature of the fighting and the fact that the British had introduced reinforcements on Thursday. It was a tribute to the fortitude of the Volunteers that the British seriously overestimated their numerical strength at a time when they could in fact have overwhelmed them by sheer weight of numbers. In the end, the South Dublin Union garrison yielded only as part of the general surrender.

———

All over the city heavy fighting continued. At the small garrison at Marrowbone Lane distillery, in effect an outpost between the South Dublin Union and Jacob's, a gun battle lasted all morning. Astonishingly, considering the superiority of British numbers and the fact that they effectively had the position surrounded, the British were beaten back in the early afternoon. The pressure was off for the moment.

Not so at the Four Courts, a far more important position. There, the closeness of the British cordon just behind them to the north in Brunswick Street and environs, together with the presence of artillery before them on the south quays, made their situation increasingly untenable. Gradually, the tough soldiers of the South Staffordshire regiments were deployed along the cordon and found themselves fighting a war for which they had no training. Ostensibly in the centre of a major city in the United Kingdom, they came under increasing sniper fire from unseen enemies in civilian clothes. There were casualties. And with the casualties came increasing bitterness and resentment at the unseen enemy. It was a short step from this to suspecting the entire civilian population to be complicit in the violence. Now no one was to be trusted.

The result was some of the most vicious fighting of the whole week, as combatants on both sides fought battles from house to house. These actions were to have especially tragic consequences the next day.

In the middle of the afternoon, back in the GPO, Pearse did what he did best. He rallied the garrison and gave them a speech in which he announced that the provinces had risen and that Volunteers were marching victoriously to the relief of the rebel city. It was a pure fiction but it served the short-term need to boost morale. It did nothing, of course, to reduce the ferocity of the artillery barrage which continued unabated.

Shortly after Pearse's address, Connolly formed a party of men and took them round to occupy the offices of the *Irish Independent* newspaper in Middle Abbey Street. He had been at this kind of thing all week: the previous day he had been across the street checking out Brennan-Whitmore's position. If Pearse was the orator, Connolly was the man of action, constantly chivvying his men, issuing orders and taking personal risks. His luck ran out on Thursday afternoon, however. Having established his men in the *Independent* office, he headed

O'Connell Street in the aftermath of the rising. (*Courtesy of the National Library of Ireland*)

back along Middle Abbey Street towards the GPO. There he caught a ricochet bullet which shattered his left shinbone. In agony, exposed and alone he managed to crawl along an alleyway to Princes Street, beside the GPO. It was here that he was found by some of his men. He was carried back inside, but he was now physically disabled. He continued to issue orders but inevitably his authority was diminished by his condition. The mere fact that he was given morphine to dull the pain was enough to see to that.

And still the British cordon tightened and still the inferno raged. Troops came down Parliament Street from the Castle with the intention of crossing to the north side and occupying Capel Street. This would have cut off the GPO from the Four Courts. The British met stout resistance from the Four Courts, despite deploying an artillery piece against its east wing. Towards midnight, to the rear of the Four Courts, the fire from the Linenhall Barracks spread to the nearby premises of a wholesale druggist, causing a series of spectacular explosions that lit up the night sky.

The scene was mirrored in Sackville Street, which now entered its death throes. Clery's department store and the Imperial Hotel were ablaze and four Volunteers who had been in occupation of the building had to leg it across the street, under a hail of bullets, to the relative safety of the GPO. One of them fell and lay still but subsequently picked himself up and reached sanctuary.

On the same side of the street, Brennan-Whitmore decided on his own initiative that his position at the head of North Earl Street was now hopeless. For one thing, Hoyle's oil refinery, which was adjacent, was an inferno, leaving Brennan-Whitmore and his men in imminent danger of being incinerated. He was perfectly ignorant of his line of retreat to the north—he did not know the city very well—but he felt that it offered the only hope.

He aimed to take his men, as he later wrote, 'through back lanes, premises, old mews and alleyways'. He formed his party of twelve into three groups of four each and slipped into Cathedral Street. Not knowing what kind of fire fight they might be heading into, they left their four female Volunteers in the sanctuary of the local presbytery—much against their will; they were more or less shoved roughly into the presbytery by the men.

The Volunteers were headed for the North Strand, where they believed that they would be safe. However, all the available streets leading to the North Strand were broad, exactly what Brennan-Whitmore had hoped to avoid. At first, they made satisfactory progress, but after about 500 yards they encountered the military. In the firing that ensued, Brennan-Whitmore and Noel Lemass were wounded. They and their party promptly occupied a ground floor room in an adjacent tenement. It was hostile territory, for the Dublin slums were full of army dependants, some of them war widows. Exhausted, Brennan-Whitmore fell asleep, despite being eaten alive by fleas.

They were duly betrayed. At first light one of the tenement women had slipped out to the British and alerted them to the Volunteers' position. Brennan-Whitmore was generous in his judgment: 'Generations of these people had, through economic necessity, gone into the British army. They knew no loyalty but to their bread and butter, or what there was of it. And they hated Sinn Féiners as the ones who were likely to deprive them of that same bread and butter.'

They were captured, were lucky not to be summarily executed—something, Brennan-Whitmore believed, would have raised a cheer from the tenement women—and were marched off to be imprisoned in the Custom House. The garrison in the GPO had not seen them slip away and believed them to have been immolated with their building. Despite their own awful extremity, they knelt down and recited a decade of the Rosary for the salvation of their colleagues' souls, at the very moment when their colleagues' bodies were being consumed by fleas.

———

All who recall that Thursday night and Friday morning remember the great fire. The centre of the city was a red glow, visible from distant suburbs on both sides of the city. The principal fires were north of the river, in Sackville Street and behind the Four Courts. The south city centre escaped, but the city's principal thoroughfare—the only street in Dublin with any pretentions to boulevard or processional status—was an inferno.

07 | FRIDAY

General Sir John Maxwell, the new commander-in-chief of British forces in Ireland, sailed into the Liffey estuary and tied up at the North Wall. It was two o'clock in the morning. Maxwell was not to play a decisive role in events until after the rising—the day-to-day direction of military affairs remained in the hands of Brigadier-General Lowe. However, before dawn he had issued this proclamation:

General Sir John Grenfell Maxwell, KC.B., K.CM.G. Proclamation:

'The most vigorous measures will be taken by me to stop the loss of life and damage to property which certain misguided persons are causing by their armed resistance to the law. If necessary I *shall not hesitate to destroy all buildings within any area occupied by the rebels and I warn all persons within the area specified below, and now surrounded by H.M. troops forthwith to leave such area under the following conditions: women and children may leave the area by any of the examining posts set up for the purpose and will be allowed to go away free. Men may take leave by the same examining posts and will be allowed to go away free provided the examining officer is satisfied they have taken no part whatever in the present disturbances. All other men who present themselves at the examining posts must surrender themselves unconditionally together with any arms and ammunition in their possession.'*

It was not the only proclamation issued that morning. With the inevitable capitulation now coming ever closer, Pearse composed a manifesto written—whether with a sense of irony or out of sheer necessity—on official Post Office stationery, complete with the royal arms.

Headquarters, Army of the Irish Republic
General Post Office, Dublin
28th April, 1916. 9.30 a.m.

The Forces of the Irish Republic which was proclaimed in Dublin, on Easter Monday, 24th April, have been in possession of the central part of the

Capital since 12 noon on that day. Up to yesterday afternoon, Headquarters was in touch with all the main outlying positions, and, despite furious, and almost continuous assaults by the British Forces all those positions were then still being held, and the Commandants in charge were confident of their ability to hold them for a long time.

During the course of yesterday afternoon and evening the enemy succeeded in cutting our communications with our other positions in the city and Headquarters is today isolated.

The enemy has burnt down whole blocks of houses, apparently with the object of giving themselves a clear field for the play of artillery and field guns against us. We have been bombarded during the evening and night by shrapnel and machine-gun fire, but without material damage to our position, which is of great strength.

We are busy completing arrangements for the final defence of Headquarters, and are determined to hold it while the building lasts.

I desire now, lest I may not have an opportunity later, to pay homage to the gallantry of the soldiers of Irish Freedom who have during the past four days been writing with fire and steel the most glorious chapters in the later history of Ireland. Justice can never be done to their heroism, to their discipline, to their gay and unconquerable spirit in the midst of peril and death.

Let me, who have led them into this, speak, in my own, and in my fellow-commanders' names, and in the name of Ireland present and to come, their praise, and ask them who come after them to remember them.

For four days they have fought and toiled, almost without cessation, almost without sleep, and in the intervals of fighting they have sung songs of the freedom of Ireland. No man has complained, no man has asked 'Why?' Each individual has spent himself, happy to pour out his strength for Ireland and for freedom. If they do not win this fight, they will at least have deserved to win it. But win it they will, although they may win it in death. Already they have won a great thing. They have redeemed Dublin from many shames, and made her name splendid among the names of cities.

If I were to mention names of individuals, my list would be a long one. I will name only that of Commandant-General James Connolly, Commanding the Dublin Division. He lies wounded, but is still the guiding brain of our resistance.

If we accomplish no more than we have accomplished, I am satisfied. I am satisfied that we have saved Ireland's honour. I am satisfied that we should have accomplished more, that we should have accomplished the task of enthroning, as well as proclaiming, the Irish Republic as a Sovereign State, had our arrangements for a simultaneous rising of the whole country, with a combined plan as sound as the Dublin plan has been proved to be, been allowed to go through on Easter Sunday. Of the fatal counter-manding order which prevented these plans from being

carried, I shall not speak further. Both Eoin MacNeill
and we have acted in the best interests of Ireland.

   For my part, as to anything I have done in this, I am
not afraid to face either the judgment of God, or the
judgment of posterity.

   (Signed) P. H. PEARSE
   Commandant-General
   Commanding in Chief, the Army of the Irish
   Republic and President of the Provisional
   Government

This was followed shortly by Connolly's final order to
his troops. He had insisted on being brought back down
into the front hall from the temporary sick bay where he
had been closeted since receiving his wound. His mere
presence, and the sense of authority and command that
he projected, raised his men's morale despite the
increasing hopelessness of their position. His order,
dictated to his ubiquitous and courageous secretary,
Winifred Carney (one of the many exceptional women
who supported the rebels and to whom Connolly pays
tribute at the end of his dispatch), bore no relation to
military reality. But that was hardly the point any more.
The rising was theatre now and Connolly, almost
assuming the mantle of a second Pearse, understood
that with the time for action passing, the time for
rhetoric had arrived.

Prisoners under escort. (© *RTÉ Stills Library*)

Army of the Irish Republic
(Dublin Command)
Headquarters, April 28th, 1916

To Soldiers,

This is the fifth day of the establishment of the Irish Republic, and the flag of our country still floats from the most important buildings in Dublin, and is gallantly protected by the officers and Irish soldiers in arms through the country. Not a day passes without seeing fresh postings of Irish soldiers eager to do battle for the old cause. Despite the utmost vigilance of the enemy we have been able to get information telling us how the manhood of Ireland, inspired by our splendid action, are gathering to offer up their lives, if necessary, in this same holy cause. We are here hemmed in because the enemy feels that in this building is to be found the heart and inspiration of our great movement.

Let us remind you of what you have done. For the first time in 700 years the flag of free Ireland floats triumphantly in Dublin City.

The British army, whose exploits we are for ever having dinned into our ears, which boasts of having stormed the Dardanelles and the German lines on the Marne, behind their artillery and machine-guns they are afraid to advance to the attack or storm any positions held by our forces. The slaughter they have suffered in the last few days has totally unnerved them, and they dare not attempt again an infantry attack on our positions.

Our Commandants around us are holding their own.

Commandant Daly's splendid exploit in capturing Linenhall barracks we all know. You must know also that the whole population, both clergy and laity, of this district are united in his praises. Commandant MacDonagh is established in an impregnable position reaching from the walls of Dublin Castle to Redmond's Hill and from Bishop Street to Stephen's Green.

(In Stephen's Green, Commandant Mallin holds the College of Surgeons, one side of the square, a portion of the other side and dominates the whole Green and all its entrances and exits.)

Commandant de Valera stretches in a position from the Gas works to Westland Row, holding the Boland's Bakery, Boland's Mills, Dublin South-eastern Railway Works and dominating Merrion Square.

Commandant Ceannt holds the South Dublin Union and Guinness's Buildings in Marrowbone Lane and controls James's Street and district.

On two occasions the enemy effected a lodgement and were driven out with great loss.

The men of North County Dublin are in the field, have occupied all the Police barracks in the district, destroyed all the telegram system on the Great Northern Railway up to Dundalk, and are operating against the trains of the Midland and Great Western.

Dundalk has sent 200 men to march upon Dublin, and in the other parts of the North our forces are active and growing.

In Galway, Captain Mellowes, fresh after his escape from an English prison, is in the field with his men. Wexford and Wicklow are strong and Cork and Kerry are equally acquitting themselves creditably. (We have every confidence that our Allies in Germany and kinsmen in America are straining every nerve to hasten matters on our behalf.)

As you know, I was wounded twice yesterday, and am unable to move about, but have got my bed moved into the firing line, and with the assistance of your officers, will be just as useful to you as ever.

Courage, boys, we are winning, and in the hour of victory, let us not forget the splendid women who have everywhere stood by us and cheered us on. Never had man or woman a grander cause, never was a cause more grandly served.

(Signed) James Connolly
Commandant-General, Dublin Division

This was the fifth day on which the tricolour of the republic was flying over public buildings in the Irish capital. It was the fifth day of armed resistance to defend that republic and that flag. Connolly's message was to resonate beyond his immediate audience and reach a wider nationalist audience. Total separation from Britain was not a fantasy: it was a serious business and

Contemporary news headlines. (*The Allen Library*)

its virtue had been asserted in blood. It was the work of serious people who were fighting a good fight. It was an honourable thing.

With every extra hour that the rebels could hold out, this message had a chance of getting through and of sinking in. The novelist James Stephens, whose diary of the rising is the most acute contemporary account, realised this early when he wrote: 'The truth is that Ireland is not cowed. She is excited a little.... She was not with the Revolution, but in a few months she will be, and her heart which was withering will be warmed by the knowledge that men have thought her worth dying for.'

All Irish nationalists disliked British rule in Ireland, and the sight of Irish men and women fighting British troops under an Irish flag was something to stir the emotions. Mixed with the horror was a tiny surge of pride. The Volunteers might be half mad, but their hearts were in the right place. Connolly's short-term fantasy would develop into long-term reality.

For most of the time since the Act of Union of 1801, nationalist Ireland—which was effectively Catholic Ireland, although with a significant Protestant influence—sought to weaken the Union and reverse its principal achievement. That had been to integrate Ireland fully into the metropolitan British state, thus creating the United Kingdom. Among its own supporters, nationalism generally sought the greatest degree of autonomy within the Union that seemed feasible at a given time. Thus O'Connell's campaign for repeal and Parnell's for home rule had many continuities. Crucially, this was as far as the Irish Catholic Church was prepared to go in support of nationalist politics, a support not made explicit until the 1880s. Beyond this consensus view stood the radicals, of whom the Fenians were the most visible group.

The Fenians were not as marginal numerically as this summary might suggest. But their radicalism, and in many cases ideological inflexibility, sat awkwardly with parliamentary politics with its compromises and pre-varications. Since Catholic Emancipation in 1829, parliament at Westminster had been the physical locus of Irish nationalist ambition. The fact that Ireland was prepared to take as much as it could get from Britain did not mean that she did not want separation. It was just that it had seemed a fantasy. What Connolly was doing was reminding his men—and all Irish nationalists—that it need not be a fantasy. Separation from Britain and a sovereign republic could be practical politics. They soon became so.

———

The position of the GPO was hopeless by mid afternoon. The roof caught fire at 4 p.m. and by evening it threatened to engulf the whole building and immolate all within. At 8, the order to evacuate the building came: Pearse and Connolly were the last to leave.

Most of the garrison left by the Henry Street exit,

heading across that street and into the warren of alleyways and lanes between it and Great Britain (now Parnell) Street. The principal street connecting Henry Street and Great Britain Street was Moore Street. It was into this street that The O'Rahilly led a group of Volunteers in a final assault on a British position at the Great Britain Street end. They were cut to pieces. O'Rahilly himself was killed. His real name was Michael Joseph O'Rahilly. He was a journalist, a Gaelic Leaguer and a founder member of the Volunteers. He had not been an IRB man and was unaware of the plans of the military council. He was of the orthodox Volunteer opinion that a rising should only be attempted when there was clear public support for it. He had spent the previous weekend driving around the provinces delivering Eoin MacNéill's countermanding order.

When he returned to Dublin, he was astonished to discover that the rising had started anyway and felt it his duty in all honour to join it. He offered himself to the GPO garrison. His death was a defining moment in how the rising was remembered, for it was gallant and courageous, quixotic even. Moreover, it helped to take the rising from the realm of theatre to that of myth. Yeats wrote a ballad about him, putting these words in his mouth:

> 'Am I such a craven that
> I should not get the word
> But for what some travelling man
> Had heard I had not heard?'

Then on Pearse and Connolly
He fixed a bitter look
'Because I helped to wind the clock
I come to hear it strike.'

Pearse and Connolly had hoped to join with Ned Daly's garrison at the Four Courts but there was no way past British positions on Capel Street. Instead, various buildings in the Moore Street area were occupied. The main body found themselves in a grocer's shop whose proprietor was a Mrs Cogan. She offered them food— boiled ham—and shelter. In the course of the night, they began to tunnel through adjacent premises in the general direction of Great Britain Street. They got as far as Hanlon's fish shop at no. 16 Moore Street.

They could go no further without abandoning Connolly, now in agony with his foot. Gangrene had set in. The business of hauling him up and down stairs and through narrow tunnelled holes made no sense. Hanlon's was as far as they got. It was from there that Pearse would walk out the following afternoon to deliver his unconditional surrender.

——

In the meantime, the remaining action was centred less than a mile away, at the rear of Daly's position at the Four Courts. The original idea behind General Lowe's cordon had been that it would run along North King

General Sir John Grenfell Maxwell. (*Courtesy of the National Library of Ireland*)

Street, only a few hundred metres north of the rear of the Four Courts itself. However, it had been occupied by some of Daly's men, who were dug in in good sniping positions in the street itself and in adjacent ones. In particular, two premises were significant in this regard. A pub called Reilly's, at the corner of North King Street and Church Street, proved a good position for rebel snipers and was afterwards mythologised as 'Reilly's Fort'. Even better was a distillery building on the corner of Beresford Street nearby, whose height was a sniper's paradise.

Lowe's cordon had to run instead along Brunswick Street, just to the north of and parallel to North King Street. The point is that the combatants were terrifyingly close to each other. Maxwell now took a hand, his one decisive operational overruling of Lowe in the course of the rising. He had troops in reserve, some of them members of the South Staffordshire regiment that had been roughed up at Mount Street Bridge earlier in the week. He ordered them in to tighten the cordon through North King Street, which would effectively strangle Daly's position in the Four Courts just down the street.

The South Staffs were in no mood for dainty soldiering. That, plus the unpredictability of the rebels—they were actually few in number, but managed to give the opposite impression—meant that the British assault descended into vicious house-to-house fighting, as the South Staffs suspected every house and tenement building of being a rebel nest. Maxwell had ordered all civilians out of the area but people had nowhere to go, least of all in the chaos that was gripping the immediate area and the city at large. Moreover, it had been the insurgents who controlled the area all week: Maxwell's writ no longer ran down there.

The local British commander at North King Street, Lt-Col Henry Taylor, resorted to rebel tactics by occupying houses and tunnelling through from one to the next in an attempt to flush out the rebels. It was a slow, wearying business and the rebels fought a clever, morale-sapping fight, leaving the British uncertain as to their positions and strength. For six hours this went on, for no British gains. The snipers on the top of the Beresford Street tower were still in action and the rebel barricade on North King Street, almost underneath it, remained solid, despite the deployment of an armoured car.

At 2 a.m. on Saturday, the South Staffs occupied no. 172 North King Street, the home of a family called Hughes. Other families had taken refuge there to escape the relentless British advance. One of them, Mrs Ellen Walsh, described what happened next.

'We heard the soldiers banging at the street door.... We then heard a voice cry "Are there any men in this house?" Immediately about thirty soldiers ... ran at us like infuriated wild beasts or like things possessed. They looked ghastly and seemed in a panic. There was terrible firing going on outside in the street ... and an armoured car was near the door. One of the soldiers

with stripes on his arms seemed in command. He shouted "Hands up" and they presented their rifles at us. We all stood round the room in groups, and my husband and Mr Hughes seemed petrified at the wild looks and cries of the soldiers.... The man in command shouted "Search them" and they searched the two men and the two boys....

One of our men said "There was no one firing from this house". The corporal with stripes said "Not firing, eh?" and pointing to a rip in his hat said "Look what a bullet did for me. I nearly lost my life." The women and children were then all ordered down into the back kitchen and my poor husband and Mr Hughes were brought upstairs. I'll never forget the horror of it. Some time after I heard a voice upstairs crying "Mercy! Mercy! Don't put that on me" and someone resisting as if being tied up, or having his eyes bandaged. The old man in the upper room close by heard my husband crying, and as they killed him they heard his last words: "O Nellie, Nellie jewel.")'

The unfortunate men who were killed were joined by thirteen more before the night was out. It was dawn before the North King Street barricade was finally overrun but its conquerors were still caught between fire from Reilly's Fort on one side of them and the distillery tower above them. The frontal assault on the rebel position at North King Street was claiming a horrible toll in both military and civilian lives. It was not until 9 a.m. on Saturday that the half-dozen remaining

Volunteers in Reilly's decided to pack it in. They were painfully short of ammunition: an attempt to run down Church Street to get more from Daly had simply resulted in the death of the Volunteer who was carrying it.

In all, the battle had taken sixteen hours and had brought the most concentrated fighting of the entire rising, albeit the aggregate casualties were not as great as at Mount Street Bridge on Wednesday. But it was the end. There was nothing left now but the surrender.

08 | SATURDAY AND AFTER

The position in no. 16 Moore Street was hopeless. The remains of the GPO garrison were holed up there, with no realistic hope of escape. A plan to make a run for it down Henry Street was contemplated and abandoned. Then, burning embers from the gutted GPO set fire to a nearby pub. The owner, his wife and daughter fled their burning premises under cover of a white flag. It did not save them. They were gunned down by the British.

It was this incident—and the certainty that further resistance was sure to entail more loss of civilian life—that prompted Pearse to order the surrender.

At 12.45 p.m., Nurse Elizabeth O'Farrell, part of the women's auxiliary that had loyally stood by their posts in a number of Volunteer commands all week, issued out in to Moore Street wearing Red Cross markings and carrying a white flag. She was met at the British barricade at the end of the street by an officer to whom she said: 'The commandant of the Irish Republican Army wishes to treat with the commandant of the British forces in Ireland.'

The officer was perplexed. 'The Irish Republican Army? The Sinn Féiners, you mean.'

'No', she replied, 'the Irish Republican Army they call themselves and I think that is a very good name too.'

Nurse O'Farrell was held in a nearby shop—irony of ironies, it was Tom Clarke's tobacconists—to await the arrival of Brigadier-General Lowe, who materialised in due course. He sent her back to Pearse with the message that only unconditional surrender was acceptable and that Pearse had a ceasefire of half an hour, no more.

At 2.30 p.m. Lowe received Pearse at the top of Moore Street. Pearse handed his sword to Lowe. He was taken off to meet Maxwell. Connolly was removed to a Red Cross station in Dublin Castle to have his wound treated. At 3.45 Pearse signed the following surrender order: 'In order to prevent the further slaughter of Dublin citizens, and in the hope of saving the lives of our followers now surrounded and hopelessly outnumbered, the members of the Provisional Government present at headquarters have agreed to an unconditional surrender, and the commandants of the various districts in the city and country will order their commands to lay down arms.'

The men of the GPO garrison were marched to the top of Sackville Street beside the Parnell monument and

The protracted executions made for compelling if grisly copy. (*The Allen Library*)

then corralled in the gardens of the Rotunda maternity hospital. Nurse O'Farrell, meanwhile, was given the task of conveying the surrender order to the various outlying garrisons. At Boland's Mills and Jacob's, the respective commanders, de Valera and MacDonagh, had taken some convincing that the surrender was not a hoax. They had been remote from the action for seventy-two hours in de Valera's case and for the whole week in MacDonagh's. The latter eventually got word to Ceannt in the South Dublin Union and to the Volunteers in Marrowbone Lane.

The men in the Rotunda garden spent the night in the open before being marched to Richmond Barracks the following morning. They got a hostile reception in some of the tenement quarters through which they passed. The official casualty list reckoned 1,351 people dead or badly wounded—the majority of them non-combatants. The city centre, especially just north of the river, was devastated. Over 100,000 people needed public relief.

——

The remark made by the British officer to Nurse Elizabeth O'Farrell when she first approached the barricade under a flag of surrender told a lot. 'The Sinn Féiners, you mean?' To the British, it was the Sinn Féin rebellion right from the start. Sinn Féin, in fact, had nothing to do with it. It was a small, radical nationalist group—one of many, and by 1916 by no means the most important or influential—that proliferated in nationalist Ireland in the years before the Great War. Its leading spirit was Arthur Griffith, a journalist. He was a cultural and economic nationalist and a political radical, being both a Fenian and a member of the Gaelic League.

He had made his name in 1904 by publishing a proposal entitled 'The Resurrection of Hungary' in which he praised the *Ausgleich* of 1867 which split the Hapsburg empire into two spheres of influence, thus turning what had been the Austrian empire into the Austro-Hungarian empire. He proposed a similar Anglo-Irish arrangement. Whatever this was, it was not republicanism or anything like it. None the less, the early Sinn Féin—it was founded in 1905—attracted attention, partly because of Griffith's talent as a propagandist and partly because of its dislike of the Irish Parliamentary Party. It ran candidates in by-elections and performed creditably, offering a form of radical alternative to the IPP for a while. But in the ferment surrounding home rule in the years preceding the war, it looked as if Redmond had won his point. Sinn Féin, in common with other radical nationalist groups, appeared to have shot their bolt.

And in a sense they had. But their name had entered the political vocabulary as a generic for all versions of nationalism to the left of the IPP—and the name stuck. So it was that in the aftermath of the rising, the British erroneously disinterred a name that might otherwise have sunk into historical obscurity. On the basis that if the cap fits wear it, Sinn Féin became the omnibus term for all whose politics supported and celebrated the rising. From this time until the new Sinn Féin supplanted the IPP as the definitive voice of Irish nationalist politics in the general election of 1918, there was an internal contest for the soul of Irish nationalism. It was largely generational, with youth tending to Sinn Féin and age sticking with the party.

This was an unexpected side effect of the Great War. The emigration routes, which had been full of young Irish in every decade since the Great Famine of the 1840s, were closed for the duration of the conflict. Many of the most able and energetic, who might previously have sought a better life abroad, were now bottled up in Ireland. Their presence was, at a minimum, a contributory factor in the radicalisation of the nationalist demand. Indeed, the Great War was the indispensable context for the rising. The instability it created and the old cry that 'England's difficulty is Ireland's opportunity' were irresistible.

The Sinn Féin that emerged from the rising was quite unlike the pre-war version. It quickly became a mass party and within a few years was to dominate nationalist politics. When it split in 1922 over the terms of the Anglo-Irish Treaty, its constituent elements formed the basis of the two dominant political parties in what is now the Republic of Ireland. Sinn Féin itself—or a version of it (it is a protean entity)—still exists, and is the junior partner in the Northern Ireland Executive.

——

Roger Casement during his trial. (*The Allen Library*)

Once the rising had been put down, the question arose of what to do with the leaders. General Maxwell was now the man of the hour. He was in his fifties, a soldier with no more political sophistication than most of his kind, whose career was stalled until this moment. His country was engaged in a life-or-death struggle in Europe and the war was not going well. To his way of thinking, the matter was simple. The rebels had conspired with the German enemy and the rising was nothing more or less than a stab in the back. Ireland was properly part of the United Kingdom; its people owed a duty of allegiance to lawful authority, all the more so in wartime; those who defied this duty deserved condign punishment.

Many voices pleaded with him. John Dillon, deputy leader of the IPP, spoke passionately in the House of Commons against any policy of executing the leaders of the rising. The influential Bishop of Limerick, Dr O'Dwyer, spoke out likewise. So did George Bernard Shaw and others. Maxwell was unmoved. A series of military courts martial were constituted, the first of which sat on 2 May and sentenced Pearse, Clarke and MacDonagh to death. The sentences were carried out the following day.

All the garrison leaders, with the single exception of de Valera, were executed. But not just the garrison leaders: Willie Pearse, Patrick's younger brother, appears to have been shot for no better reason than he was who he was. In all fifteen men were shot in a gruesomely drawn-out tragedy that dragged on until the twelfth. On that day, James Connolly, unable to stand, was executed while sitting on a chair in the military hospital in Dublin Castle.

On the same day, the prime minister, H.H. Asquith, came to Ireland and re-established political control of the situation. By then, it was abundantly clear that all the warnings from Shaw and others about the effect that the executions would have were coming true. Because of its circumstances, Connolly's death caused particular public revulsion. But there was no undoing the damage that had been done. It would be wrong to say that the executions lost Ireland for England—because in truth she had been emotionally lost long since, inasmuch as there had ever been any more than a resigned and fatalistic acceptance of crown rule—but they were another nail in the coffin of the legitimacy of British rule in Ireland.

De Valera escaped the firing squad in circumstances that have been disputed. Having been born in New York, he could claim US citizenship. The fear of antagonising American opinion was traditionally proposed as the reason for his escape. However, the crown prosecutor at the courts martial, Lt W.E. Wylie, records that de Valera was saved by the growing political pressure arising from the earlier executions. Maxwell showed him a telegram from Asquith that sought a mitigation of the execution policy, at least to ensure that only prominent ringleaders were shot. He enquired of Wylie as to who was next on the list to be tried.

'Somebody called de Valera, sir,' said Wylie.

'Who is he? I haven't heard of him before.'

Wylie told him what little he knew of de Valera, to which Maxwell replied, 'I wonder would he be likely to make trouble in the future?'

'I wouldn't think so sir, I don't think he is important enough. From all I can hear he is not one of the leaders.'

There is no reason to doubt Wylie's testimony. He was there. He went on to have a distinguished career as a judge and his word is as close as we are likely to get to the inside details of the moment. Wylie's judgment of de Valera was one of the great misreadings of an individual in modern Irish history. Dev went on to make a lot of trouble in the future, and to dominate independent Ireland until the mid century.

More than 3,500 people were arrested in the aftermath of the rising, many of them on very poor intelligence. Almost half were released without charge within two weeks. Most of the others were interned, many of them in Frongoch in Wales. In the classic way of these things, Frongoch turned out to be a revolutionary university. Many of those who made the Irish revolution in the coming years were there. Michael Collins became the best-known of them.

———

In the end, how do we sum the whole thing up? It was a pure revolutionary conspiracy. The military council was a self-appointed conspiratorial body which hid its

The execution yard in Kilmainham Gaol. (© *RTÉ Stills Library*)

plans from the Irish Volunteers and the IRB alike. It is hard to imagine that they could have succeeded in their plans even if the original mobilisation had gone ahead on Easter Sunday. But the loss of German arms off the Kerry coast and the countermanding order by Eoin MacNéill removed whatever slim hope there was of anything that could be represented as a military victory.

None the less, there was something strangely old-fashioned about the Easter Rising of 1916, something looking back to the nineteenth century. The occupation of public buildings and the erection of barricades were reminiscent of the revolutions of 1848 or the Paris Commune of 1870. These dispositions were a passive invitation to counter-attack. The contrast with the War of Independence a few years later was total. The war was concentrated in the countryside, using hit-and-run guerrilla tactics and an energetic propaganda machine on the political side.

The Easter Rising of 1916 was never intended to produce military victory or the immediate end of British rule in Ireland. It was a theatrical gesture and a cry to save what the rebels regarded as Ireland's lost honour. They were men and women of their time. Much of the talk of blood and conflict and honour that rang throughout Europe in the fin de siècle found an echo in Irish nationalist rhetoric as well. Pearse and Kipling were not as far apart as might first appear. To Pearse and the other separatists, the compromises and accommodations of the Irish Parliamentary Party—the essential grist of work-a-day politics—represented a form of national humiliation. To them, these politicians were trimmers and temporisers: they were local patrons and bigwigs with a political clientele of the comfortable and the satisfied. The young men who made the rising were little interested in politics or in political accommodation, although ironically Pearse himself had been prepared to accept the terms of a very anodyne measure known as the Irish Council Bill as recently as 1907. The radicalisation of Pearse's politics in the ten years prior to the rising found an echo in many others of his generation.

The rising was not simply a middle-class affair, although it was that. It was rather bohemian and exotic. Pearse, Plunkett and MacDonagh were not ordinary bourgeois: they were part of an intellectual and literary subset of the nationalist middle class. McDermott and Clarke were revolutionary activists through and through: having helped to trigger the rising, they were relatively passive members of the GPO garrison. Likewise Plunkett, who was debilitated by the disease that was consuming him. Connolly was a revolutionary socialist.

At some point, mainstream nationalist opinion, or at least mainstream middle-class nationalist opinion, was bound to reassert itself. For a few years the myth created by the martyrs of 1916 threw a blanket over nationalist life that concealed a lot. Only under the pressure of the Treaty debates in 1922 did some of the underlying tensions and divisions reappear. The working class was sidelined altogether. The Treaty was supported for the most part by the settled and the comfortable in Irish life and was opposed in disproportionate numbers by the marginalised.

There is, of course, an irony here. It was radicals and exotics that made the great mythical event that was the rising. They were revered in iconic images: Pearse's photograph in profile hung like a sacred icon in many an Irish kitchen. But the shabby genteel, petty bourgeois reality of the state that eventually emerged was disconnected from every kind of adventurous radicalism. It was a world made safe for small farmers and small businesses and small minds, where censorship was quickly imposed and divorce was quickly forbidden. It was a state in which the suffocating moral authority of the Catholic Church went unchallenged, indeed was positively celebrated.

Irish nationalist democracy traced its origins to the heroic foundation event of Easter Week, to the challenge in arms against the might of England. But that event was kept at a considerable mental distance from the reality of post-1922 Ireland. In a sense, that's how it was fated to be. The rising represented no identifiable constituency and had no political legitimacy in the ordinary sense of the term. It was never intended to be part of grubby quotidian reality. Indeed, it proposed itself in total opposition to the prevailing version of that reality, as expressed at the time by the Irish Parliamentary Party. But that reality was rooted in the sociology of the Land Acts that created the network of small farms and small towns in a society that had not yet industrialised. This social reality had to find its voice sooner or later. In all this, there is an ironic posthumous apotheosis for Pearse and the others. They had intended the rising as theatre, as symbol, as myth. And that is precisely what it became in the eyes of later generations, an enabling myth, something heroic to which the very ordinary and unambitious state that emerged from it and from subsequent events could look up to as a symbolic ideal.

And it did change the political weather for ever. For nearly a week the tricolour flag had flown over the GPO. It flies there today and it is inconceivable that any other flag should fly in its place. Had Ireland merely got home rule, the union flag would still have been in place. It might seem a small thing, the symbolism of flags, but it is not.

SELECT BIBLIOGRAPHY

— Bew, Paul, *Ireland: the politics of enmity 1789–2006*, Oxford University Press 2007

— Bew, Paul, *Ideology and the Irish Question: Ulster unionism and Irish nationalism 1912–1916*, Oxford: Clarendon Press 1994

— Boyce, D.G., *Nineteenth-Century Ireland: the search for stability*, Dublin: Gill & Macmillan 1990

— Boyce, D.G., ed., *The Revolution in Ireland 1879–1923*, Dublin: Gill & Macmillan 1988

— Brennan-Whitmore, W.J., *Dublin Burning: the Easter Rising from behind the barricades*, Dublin: Gill & Macmillan 1996

— Caulfield, Max, *The Easter Rebellion*, Dublin: Gill & Macmillan 1995

— Comerford, R.V., *Ireland: inventing the nation*, London: Hodder Arnold 2003

— Connolly, S.J., ed., *The Oxford Companion to Irish History*, Oxford University Press 1998

— Doherty, Gabriel and Keogh, Dermot, eds, *1916: the long revolution*, Cork: Mercier Press 2007

— English, Richard, *Irish Freedom: the history of nationalism in Ireland*, London: Macmillan 2006

— Ferriter, Diarmaid, *The Transformation of Ireland 1900–2000*, London: Profile Books 2004

— Foster, Roy, *Modern Ireland 1600–1972*, London: Allen Lane, The Penguin Press 1988

— Garvin, Tom, *Nationalist Revolutionaries in Ireland 1858–1928*, Oxford University Press 1987

— Hegarty, Shane and O'Toole, Fintan, *The Irish Times Book of the 1916 Rising*, Dublin: Gill & Macmillan 2006

— Hickey, D.J. and Doherty, J.E., *A New Dictionary of Irish History from 1800*, Dublin: Gill & Macmillan 2003

— Jackson, Alvin, *Home Rule: an Irish history 1800–2000*, London: Weidenfeld & Nicolson 2003

— Jackson, Alvin, *Ireland 1798–1998*, Oxford: Blackwell 1999

— Jeffery, Keith, *Ireland and the Great War*, Cambridge University Press 2000
— Killeen, Richard, *A Short History of the Irish Revolution 1912–1927*, Dublin: Gill & Macmillan 2007
— Killeen, Richard, *The Concise History of Modern Ireland*, Dublin: Gill & Macmillan 2006
— Lee, J.J., *Ireland 1912–1985: politics and society*, Cambridge University Press 1989
— McGee, Owen, *The IRB: the Irish Republican Brotherhood from the Land League to Sinn Féin*, Dublin: Four Courts Press 2005
— Moody, T.W., ed., *The Fenian Movement*, Cork: Mercier Press 1968
— Ó Broin, León, *W.E. Wylie and the Irish Revolution 1916–1921*, Dublin: Gill & Macmillan 1989
— O'Brien, Conor Cruise, *States of Ireland*, London: Hutchison 1972
— O'Brien, Conor Cruise, ed., *The Shaping of Modern Ireland*, London: Routledge & Kegan Paul 1960
— O'Halpin, Eunan, *The Decline of the Union: British government in Ireland 1892–1920*, Dublin: Gill & Macmillan 1987
— Stephens, James, *The Insurrection in Dublin*, Gerrards Cross: Colin Smythe 1992
— Townshend, Charles, *Easter 1916: the Irish rebellion*, London: Allen Lane 2005
— Townshend, Charles, *Political Violence in Ireland: government and resistance since 1848*, Oxford: Clarendon Press 1983

INDEX